ADRIENNE LECOUVREUR

THE ACTRESS
AND THE
AGE

A Biography

BY JACK RICHTMAN

PRENTICE-HALL, INC.
❖ *Englewood Cliffs, New Jersey* ❖

Design by Linda Huber

ADRIENNE LECOUVREUR: The Actress and the Age
by Jack Richtman
Copyright © 1971 by Jack Richtman
All rights reserved. No part of this book
may be reproduced in any form or by any means
except for the inclusion of brief
quotations in a review, without permission
in writing from the publisher.
ISBN: 0-13-008698-3
Library of Congress Catalog Card Number: 76-164920
Printed in the United States of America   T
Prentice-Hall International, Inc., London
Prentice-Hall of Australia, Pty. Ltd., Sydney
Prentice-Hall of Canada, Ltd., Toronto
Prentice-Hall of India Private Ltd., New Delhi
Prentice-Hall of Japan, Inc., Tokyo

Acknowledgments

I WISH TO ACKNOWLEDGE MY
gratitude to the following persons and institutions
whose assistance and services were essential
to the completion of this book:

Archives of the Comédie-Française
Bibliothèque Nationale, Paris
Bibliothèque de l'Arsenal, Paris
The New York Public Library
The Libraries of Columbia University
*The Library of the State University of New York
at Albany*
*The United States Educational Commission
for France*
Professor Gita May, Columbia University
Professor Otis Fellows, Columbia University

J.R.
Provincetown,
Massachusetts.

Table of Contents

Chapter One

INTRODUCTION

OME NAMES LIVE *and may be spoken of at each moment as if they were present. . . . They are known by all, and yet one is still curious to hear them spoken, always with the hope of learning more about them. Glamour, romance, a fate full of excitement, devotion, tenderness, a touching misfortune, are what cling to those poetic figures and which, once handed down and time-honored, obtain for them a continued rejuvenation in the imagination of succeeding ages. Around them an undying legend is formed. If the location of their tombs were known, wreaths would be piously laid. Adrienne Lecouvreur is one of these names.*

In the middle of the last century, the eminent critic Sainte-Beuve thus began his review of a new play by Scribe and Legouvé—those brilliant French dramatists of bourgeois morality—entitled *Adrienne Lecouvreur*. For Sainte-Beuve's time, Adrienne Lecouvreur was perhaps the epitome of the impassioned, suffering, and betrayed woman, the heroine of the *comédie de moeurs*, which must have reached one of its heights in 1849 with this production. The play was at once a sensationalized

13

version of her romantic life and the mystery of her death, and this was reason enough for Sainte-Beuve to attempt to evoke a more accurate picture of the actress. Stressing the important role she played in bringing about a quiet revolution in acting style, he spoke of her principal merits: everything that is the very opposite of declamation.

In fact, these merits had already been recognized by not a few of Adrienne's early eighteenth-century contemporaries. The *Mercure de France* praised her for having introduced the simple and natural style of acting and for having done away with chanted declamation. François-Marie Arouet de Voltaire, one of her close friends, had written an "Epître à Mademoiselle Lecouvreur" in which he extolled her eminent qualities in the theatre, particularly her naturalness. Shortly after her death, her first biographer, the dramatic author Léonor-Jean-Christine Soulas, Abbé d'Allainval, gave the basic facts of her life. In the form of a letter to an English friend, d'Allainval reminded him—and thereby us—that from among the wonders of Paris, four were especially worthy of remembrance: the Tuileries, the dancing of Camargo, the voice of Mlle LeMaure, and the acting of Adrienne Lecouvreur.

Later on, long after her death and the end of the Old Régime, historians were among the first to succumb to her appeal. In 1823 she was eulogized before a plenary meeting of the Académie-Française by the respected historian Pierre-Edouard Lemontey. Jules Michelet, in his *Histoire de France*, spoke of her with none of the usual cold impartiality of the critic and historian. But it was not until 1887 that the actor Régnier de la Brière, turned historian of the theatre, published a penetrating study of her art which, by 1892, had attracted the attention of Georges Monval, the archivist of the Comédie-Française. Monval succeeded in locating many of Adrienne's letters, including important hitherto unknown and unpublished documents, which he then published in a small volume entitled *Lettres d'Adrienne Lecouvreur*.

At once biographers and historians set to work, capitalizing on those aspects of the letters which best suited their intentions. In so doing, they tended toward romanticizing the facts, often ending by completely distorting them, and neglecting what are probably the most significant features in the life and professional career of Adrienne Lecouvreur: her contribution to the art of acting, and her acceptance by a society noted for its total disdain of members of her profession.

That Adrienne Lecouvreur loved Maurice de Saxe, the most brilliant warrior of his day; that she inspired Voltaire, the greatest poet of the period, to write his most touching elegy; that she was *perhaps* the victim of a vicious crime; that she was refused a place of burial by the Church—thus causing public outrage—are well-documented aspects of a brilliant career. But since the publication of her correspondence—which showed her to be a prolific and strikingly appealing letter-writer—there has been no serious discussion of this remarkable lady of the theatre. Except for several published comments on Monval's work and the publication of her remaining letters (those written to Maurice de Saxe) in 1926 and 1927, there has been no attempt to place her in historical perspective. It is noteworthy that in 1956 the eminent French bimonthly, the *Revue des Deux Mondes*, published a long article based on Adrienne's life, and that as recently as

15

1960 there were two full-length historical novels dealing with this distinguished tragedienne, whose authors did nothing more than perpetuate the legend of her romantic life and spectacular death.

The demand for these last-mentioned books appears to have come about as a result of the many performances and expensive new productions, in New York and abroad, of Francesco Cilea's opera *Adriana Lecouvreur,* whose libretto is based on the Scribe and Legouvé play. These two gentlemen had altered even the *known* historical facts to fit the demands of politics at the advent of Louis-Napoléon, as well as the personal requirements of their leading lady, the great Rachel. A half-century later another actress, considering Scribe and Legouvé's work outmoded and shopworn, wrote her own full-length version of the drama and performed it for several seasons at the theatre which bore her name: Sarah Bernhardt.

All this has resulted in a mixture of fact and fantasy which the public has generally accepted as truth, thus making Adrienne Lecouvreur into an archetype-personified of romantic passion. The historical Adrienne Lecouvreur is certainly more interesting, however: she achieved all the success possible in her profession without making any essential sacrifice to the prejudices of her time. She was the public's favorite, yet she did not feel obliged to cater to its taste for the pretentious, affected, and histrionic manner of conduct, whether on or off the stage. Perhaps we shall never be able to define satisfactorily what has been referred to as her simple, natural, and noble style of acting. Whatever her particular approach, she brought a new orientation to acting style which served as a model for future generations of actresses, representing a complete change from what had gone before.

Her correspondence contains several exquisite pages. Indeed, on one or two occasions the depth of her emotion caused her to attain the highest level of eloquence, even if placing her name alongside that of a Madame de Sévigné would be to lend to her writing a pretension that she herself would have rejected.

She once complained to a friend who had been neglectful in his correspondence: "Why do you hesitate sending me news of yourself? I do not expect an *épître* fit for publication. If you allow yourself to succumb to this ill-founded fear, what do you suppose I should do, poor writer that I am? When it concerns my friends, it never enters my mind that I need great wit to write to them." In the final analysis, the personal value of her correspondence is superior to its literary merit; for incontestably, what is best in her letters is herself.

Her rise in society was equal to her success in the theatre. No actress on the French stage before her could claim such a distinction. Endowed with the virtues of the *honnête-homme*, she took quite seriously the ideals of love, friendship, generosity, and loyalty—and this at the height of the Regency, when skepticism was fashionable and the nonmaterial aspects of existence were generally scoffed at.

In the desire to remove our subject from the realm of fantasy where she has long been misrepresented, place her in the domain of history where she has long been neglected, and thus make a modest but useful contribution to the history of the theatre, we have perhaps uncovered an Adrienne Lecouvreur for our own time. Having lived in that age of fantasy, impropriety, and *dérègle-ment* which had its direct roots in the Regency following the death of Louis XIV and was to continue until the French Revolution, Adrienne Lecouvreur, by her dynamic personality, intelligence, and troubled life, was a person to be reckoned with. This *fille du peuple* who refused to be the *fille galante* made herself an emancipated woman in absolute possession of her person.

Did not this personal revolution contain within it the essence of protest that was to culminate in 1789? For us at least, Adrienne Lecouvreur is the symbol of a destiny self-created.

Chapter Two

THE RUE DES MARAIS
1692–1707

I N TODAY'S PARIS a short street called the rue Visconti runs parallel to the Seine and to the Boulevard Saint-Germain. Although the elegant homes on the neighboring streets have long since given way to gleaming storefronts, expensive apartments, and fashionable business establishments, the rue Visconti has hardly changed since it was first laid out in the early fifteenth century. It was then known as the rue des Marais-Saint-Germain, which name it kept until the middle of the nineteenth century.

Strolling down the rue Bonaparte from the Boulevard Saint-Germain and approaching rue Visconti on the right, one notices that the corner house is decorated with a small plaque informing the passerby that Jean Racine died here—on a balmy Spring morning, which the plaque does not tell—in the year 1699.

In the last year of the seventeenth century, Paris was still a city with a medieval character: overcrowded, dirty, noisy. Half of her populace lived in the streets, and most of the rest in one-room hovels; a small minority of clergy, professionals, and aristocracy inhabited palaces, mansions, and modest homes of the type in which Racine lived. Yet even then Paris was the city most associated

19

with the history of France: the city of the League, of the Fronde, of the Guises, of the Medici, of the Valois. Not yet the city of the grand and stately boulevards, its most important thoroughfares were tortuous and sinuous, winding streets where two carriages could pass each other only at certain intervals.

But on April 21, 1699, the narrow street where Racine had the last of his many Paris residences was encumbered by a surprising number of coaches of the court in all their dazzling splendor. Great ladies thronged Racine's modest antechamber: Mary Hamilton, Comtesse de Gramont, was especially noted for the abundance of her tears. Though Louis XIV hated and strove to ignore all that was ominous or gloomy, he nonetheless sent daily to inquire and was convinced the poet would pull through. A narrower circle visited the quiet sick-room: the critic Nicholas Boileau-Despréaux, of course, who had lately gone deaf; Drs. Félix and Dodart were in constant attendance. According to modern estimates, they were no great men of science, but they were gentlemen of experience and sense.

Racine's last wish was that he be buried in the cemetery of the abbey in the fields, Port-Royal-des-Champs, the hotbed of Jansenist doctrine, near Paris. The King granted his request. Had not Racine, after all, renounced the theatre some twenty-two years earlier after the success of his greatest tragedy, *Phèdre*, in order to become official "historiographer" to the King? Was it not only at Madame de Maintenon's insistence that he wrote his two last plays—on biblical themes—*Esther* and *Athalie* in 1689 and 1691? Although this was the time when members of the theatrical profession were refused the right of being buried in consecrated ground, Racine would escape the fate of Molière who, in 1673, had been fatally stricken while performing in his last play—ironically, *le Malade Imaginaire*. After many pleas by his wife and close friends, Molière's remains were finally accorded "a piece of ground" by his royal benefactor, Louis XIV.

Some thirty-one years after Racine's death, the rue des Marais was to witness the demise of another great member of the profession. There would be no piece of ground for her, however. Instead, her body would be dissolved upon a bed of quicklime. But on the day of Racine's death, in whose tragedies she would grasp the sensibility of an entire nation as though it were a dying torch and raise it to an unfamiliar, yet lifegiving realm, Adrienne Lecouvreur was but seven years old.

She was born on the 5th of April, 1692, in the village of Damery in the province of Champagne, quite near Epernay. Given her godmother's name, she was officially legalized and recorded in the following manner:

> On 5 April 1692, was born and baptized
> Adrienne, daughter of Robert Couvreur and
> Marie Bouly, father and mother; godfather, Pierre
> Dury; godmother, Adrienne Laurent; the
> father was present. Signed: Adrienne Laurent;
> Robert Couvreur.

Robert Couvreur, a worker in a hat-making establishment, took his family shortly thereafter to the large town of Fismes, between Rheims and Soissons, in the hopes of making a better living. Unsuccessful after ten years, he moved his family again, this time to Paris, where Couvreur hoped to have more lucrative opportunities in hat-making. Alas, wigs were still very much in vogue in the early part of the eighteenth century, but Couvreur's move did prove fortunate for reasons that had nothing to do with millinery. By chance he lodged his family in a cellar located in the immediate vicinity of the Comédie-Française, which then had its theatre on the rue des Fossés-Saint-Germain-des-Prés (today's rue de l'Ancienne-Comédie).

Adrienne's memories of her family were marked with bitterness.* She was to describe the hovel she shared with her family as the abode of "bitterness, anger, and rank madness." This was hardly an exaggeration: her father, mentally unbalanced since his days at Fismes, eventually would be committed to an asylum. All too early Adrienne had felt the strength of his hand. Nor was her mother, who vented her own frustrations on the child, any kinder. Three to four times daily Adrienne was beaten by this unhappy woman. During the *ancien-régime*, when child-training was of strict authoritarian vintage and blows were given out freely, life was difficult for most children, and Adrienne learned to accept her situation. But with the birth of her younger sister Marie-Marguerite in 1705, the family's poverty worsened. Marie Couvreur's death, a short time later, gave widower Robert reason to frequent the taverns, and his drunken rages bore ample evidence of his approaching insanity. To escape his constant persecution, the adolescent Adrienne would slip out into the street.

It would appear, therefore, that her precocious understanding of French tragedy was self-acquired. Even when

---

* For a delightful résumé of Adrienne's early years and young womanhood, see: "Born for Tragedy" by Florence Stevenson, in *Opera News*, February 9, 1963.

very young she had delighted friends in Fismes by reciting scraps of verse, and it is certainly possible that the darkened auditorium of the Comédie-Française afforded her a refuge; that watching the actors in rehearsal stimulated her passion for the theatre. For a short time she had attended the school of a sisterhood called the Filles d'Instruction Chrétienne, located on the rue du Gindre, close to the Couvreurs' lodgings. When she was thirteen, however, a chance circumstance pointed the way to her theatrical vocation.

Several young people of the neighborhood—runaway teenagers of questionable origin or, like Adrienne, children of a laboring class of artisans with enough sensitivity to seek out the make-believe world of the stage—decided to earn money by performing plays. They began to meet for rehearsals in the back room of a grocer's shop on the rue Férou. With Adrienne in the role of Pauline, the youthful troupe gave so worthy a performance of Pierre Corneille's *Polyeucte* that word quickly spread throughout the quarter, finally reaching the attention of Madame du Gué, the wife of a president of *Parlement*. She offered the little troupe the use of the inner courtyard of her mansion on the rue Garancière and invited many of her important friends to an evening of entertainment, which would include a performance of *Polyeucte* to be followed by one of Thomas Corneille's (Pierre's brother) light comedies incongruously entitled *Le Deuil*.

Madame's friends were likely to accept, if only out of boredom. The last years of Louis XIV's reign lent little enough éclat to the early part of the eighteenth century. But notwithstanding the defeats of his armies, the disasters of his navy, the loss of a portion of his conquests, the

23

dilapidation of his finances, and the suffering of his sub-jects, the aged monarch still sustained his great place among the sovereigns of Europe. In his last hours, he must have foreseen that the institution of monarchy, which he had raised to such a pitch of grandeur and prosperity, was likely to join him in the grave.

Toward the close of this reign which had opened so brilliantly and terminated in the most somber monotony, the character and aspect of the French court underwent a complete change. The influence of Madame de Maintenon was the sole cause of this reversal which, beginning in 1681, became more marked as the King fell more and more under the domination of the crafty and ambitious woman whom he had married in secret—never having the courage to declare that the widow of the poet and dramatist Paul Scarron was his wife. Madame la Marquise de Maintenon had been beautiful and was still well edu-cated, clever, amusing, and five years older than the King. She established an influence over his affection and ob-tained his complete confidence. Finally she achieved com-plete supremacy: his imperious will was mastered by a real Queen who masked her power under the veil of ex-treme timidity, appearing not to take the least part in public affairs. She was sincerely devout, however, and by her piety she exercised a special authority over the King, whom she had brought to be very particular about religious observances for himself and for others.

The King's pious example effected a transformation in the court. No more fêtes or theatrical spectacles were given (Racine had fallen out of favor at court—some said because he had unthinkingly dismissed Paul Scarron as a bad dramatist in Madame de Maintenon's presence), and there was little beyond evening receptions where the guests strolled through the galleries or collected around the tables at which *ombre, hookey,* and other card games were being played. The King played with the princes and princesses and with a few persons of the household. And though Madame de Maintenon never appeared at these gatherings, her invisible personality was present, so to speak, in the conversations of the courtiers. There were a few concerts of instrumental music, and upon certain special occasions—such as victories, treaties of peace, baptisms or marriages in the royal family—singers from the theatre or the churches took part. The last ballet danced before the King was, ironically, *The Triumph of Love,* in 1681. The Royal Academy of Music, also known as the Opéra, gave its last performance before the King and court in 1685.

As to the performances of the ordinary court actors, the Comédiens du Roi, their court galas had been suppressed altogether. This was the beginning of Louis' new coldness toward his *troupe unique,* which created all sorts of difficulties for them, not the least of which was their being deprived of their theatre on the rue Guénégaud by royal decree on June 20, 1687. The late Molière's company was given three months to locate a site for a new theatre. The actors' sheer will to survive caused them to overcome almost insurmountable social and financial obstacles. Checked at every turn by the Church, they were finally authorized to purchase the site of the old Etoile tennis court on the rue des Fossés-Saint-Germain, where they constructed their new theatre and opened its doors for the first time on April 18, 1689, with *Phèdre* and *Le Médecin malgré lui.*

Still, Louis XIV honored only one theatre with his presence, namely: the theatre of the Royal School of Saint-Cyr, where the young ladies of the establishment sometimes played; for the tragedies *Esther* and *Athalie*, which Racine had written expressly for these performances, had more of a religious than a secular character.

This court, majestic rather than brilliant, seemed to have lost all recollection of what it had been some forty years before when Louis XIV, at the apogee of his glory, following the inspirations of his youth and gallantry, thought only of pleasures, fêtes, and magnificent displays to celebrate the more or less ephemeral reigns of the official mistresses (*en titre*): the Duchesse de Lavallière, the Marquise de Montespan, and Mademoiselle de Fontanges. Now equally obedient to the King's lead, the aristocracy generally avoided worldly amusements—but the King was at Versailles, and a theatrical entertainment at a private home in Paris was not so conspicuous as to become uncomfortable.

For her performance at Madame du Gué's, Adrienne draped herself in a dress borrowed from one of Madame's chambermaids. But if the dress did not fit, no one seems to have noticed. One spectator later reported that as Pauline, the untrained Adrienne charmed everyone "by a completely new manner of reciting, so natural and so true that it was unanimously agreed that she was just a short step away from becoming the greatest actress ever to appear on the French stage." We can see a trace of hindsight here, perhaps, but still it is evident that Madame's guests were pleasantly surprised. The production, however, did not end on such a reassuring note.

The Comédie-Française was invested with the exclusive

privilege of performing tragedies and comedies; a privilege which it jealously guarded, and it was quite rigorous in its persecution of offenders. And so it was that on a lovely Spring afternoon in 1705, Monsieur le Comte d'Argenson, lieutenant of police, was busy writing in his study, surrounded by full-length portraits of his ancestors, who had been famous as ambassadors of France to the Most Serene Republic of Venice. He was interrupted by his bailiff, who discreetly scratched on the door: the Dean of the Comédie-Française, accompanied by one of the actors, Monsieur Legrand, humbly begged the favor of seeing him at once.

A vigilant magistrate always ready to investigate all matters which might be considered to be of interest to the city, Monsieur d'Argenson was also well aware that the Comédiens du Roi could not be ignored—not so much because of the prestige their popularity afforded them, but more because of the important "protection" which most of the Comédie's actresses could count on in high places. He instructed his bailiff to show the callers in.

Their mission was indeed urgent. Word had reached the Comédie-Française of an "impertinent [sic] performance of *Polyeucte*" which was to be given that day in the inner courtyard of the *hôtel* of Madame la Présidente du Gué on the rue Garancière by a troupe of neighborhood children, who for some time had been rehearsing the "art of Melpomene and Thalia" in the back room of a grocer's shop on the rue Férou. Madame la Présidente had found it "piquant" to offer her friends a first glimpse of these "novice talents," and for this purpose had invited "the Court and the City." The illustrious Compagnie begged the lieutenant of police not to permit this "scandal" and

27

to ban the performance. Monsieur d'Argenson was easily convinced and put at the two delegates' immediate disposition one *exempt* and two archers, whose instructions were to accompany the two visitors to the rue Garancière and, if need be, to seize "the persons of these improvised actors."

Forcing their way past Madame du Gué's Swiss guards, they presented the horrified lady with an order for the arrest of the young people. Madame immediately sent a protest to d'Argenson. Obliged to carry out the demands of the Troupe du Roi but not wishing to offend the nobility, d'Argenson withheld the execution of his order —on condition that the performance of *Le Deuil* be called off. And this was the public's humble first contact with the actress who was later to be famous under the name of Adrienne Lecouvreur.

The Grand Prior of France, Philippe de Vendôme, however, was informed of the Comédie's persecution of Adrienne and her friends, and invited the troupe to perform within the close of the Temple, where the right of sanctuary was respected and enforced. Brother of the Duc de Vendôme, the great-grandson of Henri IV jealously guarded the rights of the ancient Temple of the Order of Malta from which—as protector of its inhabitants—he received a considerable revenue. Provided that the reason was *strictly* civil, anyone who felt persecuted by civil justice could take refuge in the Temple, and thus many merchants, tradesmen, artisans—the rough equivalent of today's small businessman—who were cruelly persecuted by corporate tyranny at that time, lived within its close. The Grand Prior of France must have likened the Comédie-Française to a persecuting corporation when he allowed the young people to take refuge there, where their small company was able to give two or three more performances before it finally disbanded.

The experience nonetheless was decisive for Adrienne. By a happy coincidence, Legrand, the same actor who had been so eager to stop the performances with armed force at Madame du Gué's, as it turns out, had his laundry done by the aunt of none other than the young offender who had played Pauline—and who by then was performing within the close of the Temple. Rushing there, he was able to glimpse the final scenes of Adrienne's last performance.

Marc-Antoine Legrand, born in 1673, was an honorable man whose good humor was sometimes greatly amusing. Short and fat, his disadvantageous physical appearance was often the key to his witticisms, and although he played the roles of tragic kings for the Comédie-Française, his audience sometimes mistook the tragedy for comedy. Once, having caused much laughter in the role of Theseus, he stopped the performance and began a thunderous harangue of the *parterre*, which he wisely concluded with several jibes at himself, ending with: "Besides, Messieurs, it is much easier for you to form yourselves into my figure than it is for me to change back to yours."

Another time, out walking with friends, he tossed several coins at a beggar who, according to custom, immediately responded by singing a *De profundis*. The jovial actor interrupted: "Really, my friend, do you take me for a corpse? Instead of your *De profundis*, it would be better if you sang *Domine salvum fac regem*, God save the king, since I play them two or three times a week." In his time, this bon vivant was also known as a playwright whose comedies and parodies were almost all successful.

He was—as so often happens—a rather mediocre actor, but a most excellent teacher.

So impressed was he with the young Adrienne that at once he asked his laundress where he might get permission to train her niece for an acting career. Robert Couvreur, whose endeavors in hat-making were by this time going from bad to worse, immediately accepted Legrand's offer.

Legrand took Adrienne to live with him in his apartment near the Couvreur lodgings and soon fell in love with her, doubtlessly in the hope that the talented teenager would replace his erstwhile mistress, who had disappeared a month earlier. Not long after Adrienne was comfortably installed, Legrand accepted a dinner invitation from a certain Marquis de Courtanvaux and was shocked to find his former mistress, in superb attire, seated beside the Marquis. Making the best of the situation, he limited himself to resignation and pleasant talk, and when taking his leave, he did not fail to return to the Marquis—and to the Marquis' *amie*, of course—an invitation for dinner several days hence.

When they arrived, Legrand humbly, and in a grave tone, requested the Marquis' permission to have a very simply dressed young girl join them at table. "Oh?" exclaimed the Marquis on seeing Adrienne, "and who is this child, my dear Amphytrion? the daughter of your cook, apparently, or of your clothes-mender?"

"Not at all," replied the actor—or so the story goes—"she is my laundress's niece; that is to say, first cousin of the beautiful lady it has pleased you to take from me, and who now reunites all my affection for her family and who alone can console me for having lost her relative."

Legrand made Adrienne work with zeal and with intelligence. Capable of giving advice that he himself did not have the talent to follow, ingenious in his ability to impart intonation and range of which he himself was incapable, he was responsible for the refinement of Adrienne's delivery, easing her more and more into that naturalness whose beginnings had charmed him from the first day on. A docile pupil, Adrienne made such surprising progress in so short a time that Legrand had no hesitation in arranging for her to perform on several of the *théâtres de société*, or private stages, which were the fashion in spite of the hostility of the Comédiens du Roi. In any case, the privileged troupe was too busy battling the *théâtres de la foire*, or fairground theatres, where performances of comedies of a serious nature were now taking place more and more frequently. Since the private stages charged no admission, the Comédie had decided to throw all its repressive strength in the direction of the fairs, thus engaging in a lengthy struggle which would eventually culminate—by way of compromise—with the invention of a new theatrical genre: the *Opéra-Comique*, a musical play with some spoken dialogue.

Adrienne's difficult tryouts before a chosen audience met with such success that Robert Couvreur was easily persuaded to let his daughter continue a career which, he knew, was all too often fatal to the virtue of its young beginners. But he knew, too, that resounding glory and important advantages could be secured by a successful few. Resolved to leave the glory to Adrienne and keep any possible advantages for himself—such as the promise of an ever-increasing income, or the possibility of important business connections—he eagerly gave Legrand per-

31

mission to seek a professional engagement for his daughter.

The actor arranged for her to meet Elisabeth Clavel, who was known as Mademoiselle Fonpré, widow of the actor Hugues-François Fonpré, and who had just been appointed director of the theatre at Lille. After a short recitation by Adrienne, she immediately assessed the girl's possibilities and hired her on the spot. Adrienne Couvreur was thereby engaged to perform in the provinces, which Legrand (who himself had played the "road" as far as Warsaw) held to be the best nursery for young talent and—more importantly—the training ground of the Comédie-Française.

As Adrienne prepared for her journey to Lille, Legrand advised her to prefix her name with the article *Le* which, resembling a nobiliary particle, has always imparted a ring of nobility to French names. Robert Couvreur sent his hats to the devil for once and for all, and with his youngest daughter in tow accompanied Adrienne to Lille.

Chapter Three

"LA FILLE GALANTE"
1707–1717

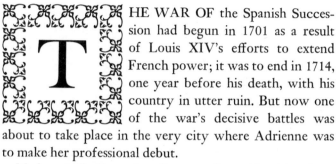HE WAR OF the Spanish Succession had begun in 1701 as a result of Louis XIV's efforts to extend French power; it was to end in 1714, one year before his death, with his country in utter ruin. But now one of the war's decisive battles was about to take place in the very city where Adrienne was to make her professional debut.

Mademoiselle Fonpré, a director of considerable talent, managed her theatre in Lille so well that it became one of the more prosperous in the provinces. The good people of Lille so appreciated the troupe that even when the Duke of Marlborough's forces bombarded and lay siege to the city in 1708, they failed to diminish attendance at performances. In fact, the bombardments were never allowed to interrupt a single representation.

Concerning the repertoires of provincial theatres of the period, there is little evidence of which plays were performed, doubtless due to the care taken by directors not to compromise their troupes for performing plays which were not their own property. As a member on leave of the Comédie-Française, Mlle Fonpré had access to that company's repertoire, and in any case was given the right to perform its comedies. In the early 1700s the chief pro-

33

viders of this genre were Dancourt, Dufresny, and the same Legrand who had introduced Adrienne to Mlle Fonpré. If comedy lacked the prestige of tragedy, it nevertheless remained the more popular genre.

As most of the plays were written while France was at war, we find in them many allusions to the fighting in Italy, Germany, and in Flanders, where Adrienne was then performing. Many of the young heroes are officers in the French army, and there are many allusions to the scarcity of males and to the difference between "winter" and "summer" lovers.* The plays concerned the manners of the lesser nobility, the bourgeoisie—large and small—servants, and peasants. Their plots varied, of course, according to the level of society and local enthusiasms, but they can usually be summed up in the following manner: an elopement is arranged by which a girl escapes from an elderly guardian and she is united to the man she loves. More often than not she is named Angélique.

Although Adrienne had been hired shortly before the siege, she had indeed made her debut to the sound of cannon fire and was an immediate success. Thus began an apprenticeship in the provinces which for Adrienne must have been a mixture of hard labor and forced pleasure. For a nature as delicate as hers, it was a life of misery. Abused by her father, tormented by her sister who had grown into a spiteful and vicious child, she craved the affection that was denied her at home. Fashionable young

---

* During the winter months a general cease-fire was customary, during which time fighting men pursued their winter loves—that is, women. During the battle season, "summer love," or homosexual love, was commonly substituted.

men and officers of the garrison made demands which soon prompted her into errors of sentiment and of conduct.

The young actor Clavel, Mlle Fonpré's brother, had just returned to the troupe after a short engagement with the Comédie-Française in Paris. Not without talent, endowed with wit and charm, he was tempted by the sixteen-year-old Adrienne's ingenuous eyes and ash-blonde hair. They lived together for a short while, but it appears that their relationship was not what could be called passionate. With a view to seeking a profitable engagement elsewhere, he took every occasion to leave town. Adrienne seems to have resigned herself to his absences, and on one such occasion, she sent the following letter to him in Paris:

> I have finally received that letter so hoped for and for which I surely must have deafened Our Lady of Carmes. I can assure you, my dear friend, that I have had no rest since your departure, due both to my concern over not hearing from you and to my worry over my present state of health. I hope that now I will improve because I have reason to believe that you still love me and that you are well. Take care of yourself, I beg you; you could give me no other pleasure since your health is as dear to me as is mine. La Dupairé [an actress in the troupe] today received a letter from Mlle Hérissé [who] says that you visit them quite often, that you are even to have supper together next Sunday. You are doing very well and I would be delighted to know that you enjoyed yourself, provided that this has nothing to

do with the reasons why I do not hear from you.
I learn by another letter that effectively you were
asked to remain in Paris and that you appeared
extremely troubled because of your having been
engaged to play for His Royal Highness. I have
no doubt that, since the writing of that letter, you
have made up your mind as you inform me in
yours; and I might as well admit that I even believe
that I am perhaps the cause. Perhaps I flatter
myself too much, but in so doing I feel that I am
giving my poor Clavel his just due. Yes, I believe
you indeed have a good heart and are thus
faithful to your poor Lecouvreur who loves you
more than she loves herself.

The news is that Mme de Léry has inherited
60,000 *écus* following the death of a 103-year-old
grandmother. Every day I receive new signs of
her kindness. She recently told me that if I had
the slightest doubt concerning you, she would
serve as your caution. Finally, she loves and
respects you infinitely and would have given you
much more tangible proof of this if you had not
been so kind and she had not been afraid to cause
gossip. These are her own words and I have added
nothing. As she is about to leave for Paris she
would like you to deliver her mules to Monsieur
Moron who is M. le Comte d'Armagnac's Swiss
guard at the King's grand stables. . . . La
Chauvert also bothered me to ask you to bring
back for her a pair of pink silk stockings and two
30-*sou* fans. I told her that you had many things
to do and that I strongly doubted that you could
lay out the funds, but she didn't understand and
simply answered that she would repay you as
soon as you return. But do what you feel best. As
far as I'm concerned I couldn't care less whether
or not you do her this favor.

Goodbye, my dear friend, I embrace you with

> all my heart and I swear my faithfulness in everything.

Adrienne's reference to her poor state of health will take on added interest for us as her career progresses. There will be many such allusions throughout her correspondence. The "Royal Highness" mentioned refers to the Prince de Condé whose Château de Chantilly contained a small theatre where performances were given for invited guests. Since Clavel was not regularly engaged with a troupe, one wonders why he was "troubled" at the prospect of Chantilly, where he doubtlessly would be well paid for his services. Even when employed in their profession, it was common for actors to seek additional financial assistance elsewhere. In the provinces the bourgeoisie was avid in its support of favorite members of the acting troupe, both male and female. Madame de Léry was doubtlessly a warm admirer of both Clavel and Adrienne, if we can judge from Adrienne's interesting reference to her as a "caution" for the assurance of Clavel's virtue. The "new signs of kindness" were most likely in the form of sums of money which were gladly accepted.

Mlle Fonpré paid her troupe very little, and out of their meager pay the actors had to supply their own costumes. Adrienne's roles required a sumptuous wardrobe, literally fit for a marquise; for already her talent seemed to destine her for the roles of tragic queen and princess in the serious tragedies, and the deceived or deceiving marquise or bourgeoise in the light comedies.

Adrienne soon acquired an expensive taste for beautiful dresses as well as for jewels and was quickly encumbered with debts. The wise, experienced Clavel soon realized that the moment had come to allow his mistress the liberty of putting her affairs in order. Through his connections he arranged for Adrienne to be engaged at the theatre at Lunéville, the brilliant provincial capital of Lorraine, where the Duc de Lorraine himself resided when resting from the still raging battles. Clavel remained in his sister's troupe at Lille. Thus, the two *amis* separated without rancor and maintained their friendship through an affectionate and regular correspondence.

Adrienne was no less successful in the sophisticated Lorraine capital than she had been in the bourgeois Flemish city: she at once became the delight of the ducal court. Handsome noblemen pursued her, and she did not repel their compliments: if we consider a certain certificate of baptism dated September 3, 1710, the warmth of her heart was all she kept for Clavel. The certificate mentions the birth of Elisabeth-Adrienne, her first child, recorded as the daughter of "Philippe Le Roy, officer of Monseigneur le Duc de Lorraine." Even though he was not asked to be godfather, Clavel did send his compliments on the event. There is no record of Philippe Le Roy after this date and, whether or not the name was real or assumed, he doubtlessly had only a brief relationship with the actress.

The Picardy regiment, which lately had become famous under Villeroi, Boufflers, and Villars, was garrisoned in the vicinity of Lunéville. It had fought gloriously in twenty battles, and its corps of officers, who had a brilliant reputation, was recruited from the noblest families of the kingdom. Although not in the service of the Duc de Lorraine, these gentlemen made the most of their proximity to Lunéville and the distraction offered by its

38

theatre. One of these choice spectators was a young nobleman whose name is a mystery. We know him simply as Baron D. Strikingly handsome, elegantly outfitted in his captain's uniform, distinguished without being stuffy, reserved without being timid, this son of a noble family was the perfect realization of the ideal hero. In fact, his friends had nicknamed him "Nemours," alluding to the character in Mme de Lafayette's novel *La Princesse de Clèves* which was still in vogue.

Actually Baron D. *was* a kind of hero, having suffered a chest wound in the battle of Ramillies. Sensible enough to contradict fashion when it went against his taste, he was of the opinion that one went to the theatre to see more than to be seen. This is why, instead of taking a seat directly on the stage among other gentlemen of fashion, he modestly preferred to watch a performance from the depth of a box, and generally alone. In this way he could fully savor his play without being disturbed by a chattering neighbor.

Even though he had steadily attended the theatre while in Lunéville, he had not yet seen the much acclaimed Lecouvreur. She had been absent for some time before and after the birth of Elisabeth-Adrienne, but Baron D., as it happened, was in the theatre when she reappeared in the role of—yes—Angélique, the unfaithful wife of Molière's *George Dandin*. So charming was she in the performance and so pretty, that Baron D. was immediately awestruck. On leaving the theatre he lost no time in making discreet inquiries about the seductive lady he had just seen perform. Each morning, he learned, it was her custom to attend the second Mass at her parish church of St. Jacques—for although automatically excommunicated because of her profession, she remained pious—and the Baron did not fail to be there the next morning. Dressed in his officer's uniform, he waited at the font by the door, and when she arrived, blonde and attractive, he bowed and offered her the holy water. Slightly surprised, she accepted, crossed herself and went to her seat.

The following morning—a fragrant summer day—the scene was repeated. Without a word being spoken, their fingers touched again. But on the third day, just as Baron D. was about to repeat the offering, Adrienne stopped him, looked squarely into his face, and smiled. "Monsieur," she said in her best stage voice, "I did not know that the priest had employed someone for the sole purpose of offering holy water." In reply he took her hand and, with no resistance from Adrienne, led her gently outside the church, where he lost no time in declaring his love, begging her pardon for having used this means to further his affections, and assuring her that from the first moment he saw her his sole desire had been to live and die in her service. So insistent was he that his words took on a singularly persuasive force.

Adrienne was already in love, even though she may not have known it then. She listened, astounded at the young officer's honesty. They strolled to the Cours Léopold, found a lonely bench in the shadow of the linden trees, and exchanged their first kiss.

From that moment the two lovers savored all the delights of a young and perfect love with all the sincerity and fire of their young ages. Each had recognized the mysterious and certain sign, that half of each seemed personified in the other. But this affection was as short-lived as it was flawless. The young baron was one of the most expert horsemen of the officer's corps. Less than a year after their first meeting, he was attempting to tame an extremely difficult horse, when he was savagely thrown. The fall ruptured the imperfectly healed chest wound he had received in the Battle of Ramillies. With massive hemorrhaging, he was taken back to his barracks, and Adrienne was hastily summoned. He died shortly after her arrival.

Adrienne had been thrown into the depths of despair, and it was feared that she would attempt to take her own life. She could not bear Lunéville, where every street revealed some reminder of this too-immediate past. In particular, the sight of the Church of St. Jacques and the Cours Léopold threw her into torrents of weeping. In a rational moment she decided to leave as quickly as possible, and before the year 1711 was out, she had signed a contract with the prosperous theatre at Strasbourg, which was also under the protection of the Duc de Lorraine.

Suffering had matured her, as well as her tragic acting-style, and now it was time to take account of herself. Before this new audience she received the acclaim to which she had been accustomed, and more and more she began to reconcile herself with life.

Having become the leading actress of the Strasbourg theatre, she earned more than 2,000 *livres* annually, an appreciable sum for the time.* But during her liaison with the young Baron D. whose allowance was far from sufficient, she had sunk even deeper into debt, and, moreover, her creditors were less than encouraged over the Baron's

* In terms of purchasing power, the *livre* might have a rough equivalent of five dollars.

death. Adrienne had often witnessed other young actresses squander their fortunes out of ignorance of how to order their lives, and she now resolved to make the necessary effort to avoid repeating her own previous errors. To do this she did not need advice, but rather a human presence, for she feared being alone. Although she had given up any idea of a new love affair, she felt the need for a companion on whom she could depend: her main concern was to give a father to her young daughter. It was therefore natural that she should think of Clavel, who had not altogether ended his relationship with her. At the beginning of Autumn in the year 1712, he could not have been too surprised to receive a letter from Adrienne. However, he certainly must have been astounded by its content: for it was nothing less than a marriage proposal:

Strasbourg, September 1712.

I hardly know what to think of your neglect, my dear Monsieur, at a time when everything appears to give me cause for alarm. My present situation gives me much time to reflect on my affairs. I ought to be the calmest person in the world and exactly the contrary is true: for I doubt that one could be more upset than I am at present, were it not for my being able to confide in no one else but you. You alone can calm all my apprehensions. What am I saying? . . . No, it would not be in your power to end them all at present. Time will either console me or afflict me even more. In the meantime, however, I shall seek from you all that can make me forget what I fear at the moment. . . . Always be assured that I love you for yourself one hundred times more

than for myself. Time will prove to you, my dear
Clavel, what I swear to you today. Always bear
the sentiments for me that I shall have for you my
whole life and this will make me happy because
this is the limit of my ambition. . . . You can see
me within two days as usual without cause for
gossip and without committing yourself. In the
final analysis you will never be forced to do what
you do not want to. As for me, with all the
inclination I have for you, I would be at the height
of despair if you did anything for me with
repugnance. Think well on it; you are still
master. Consider that I have nothing and that I
owe much, that you would find more advantage
elsewhere. All I have is my youth and good will,
but this does not pay one's bills. As you see I am
speaking frankly, and in all innocence I point out
what either will make you take me or turn away
from me. This is the moment to make your
decision. Forget propriety—in fact, you would do
me a great service by telling me your true
feelings.

I speak neither out of capriciousness nor
detachment. I love you more than ever, but I am
forced by reason to speak to you in this way. In
the name of God, do the same and never reproach
yourself for anything in my behalf. Promise
nothing that you will not carry through, even
if you must promise to hate me. That would be
kinder than to deceive me. But that was just a
manner of speaking, for I do not think you are so
ungrateful. . . . Make the decision that will
bring you the most pleasure. . . . Act as the
honorable man that you are and follow your
inclination. I will decide one way or another
whether I win or lose you. If you become mine I

43

shall have the displeasure of not making you as happy as I would like. Perhaps my happiness will make me forget that pain. . . . But no, whatever happens I shall always reproach myself for not placing you on a throne. If I lose you I will at least try not to lose you completely, and shall make it my business to remain somewhere in your esteem. If you are happy, I will have the pleasure of knowing it and of not having prevented it. If you are not happy, it at least will not have been I who was the cause, and I shall try to console myself in any way possible. . . . But take my word, for I shall perhaps never again have these sentiments, and it would be much easier if you would make your decision without delay.

Goodbye, my dear Clavel. I shall have this sent as quickly as possible for fear of regretting all I have written. Whatever decision you make, let me hear from you, and believe that I am your faithful [Lecouvreur]

Whatever gratitude Clavel may have had for Adrienne's former kindnesses, and especially after a period marked by her great love affair elsewhere, it did not extend to the point of accepting her as his wife. In fact, once Adrienne's intention became evident to him, he disappeared from sight, leaving her still without a protector and burdened with debts and a growing daughter.

As is clear from the last letter, Adrienne was after all a woman of reason, and life's experiences would thus never allow her to fall into excessive virtue. Rather than make her less attractive, tears combined with the mood of her mourning attire to make her even ravishing. She had taken to wearing mourning dress at the death of the Baron and continued the habit, knowing that black was becoming to blondes. Naturally she appeared on stage in her various costumes, so that those who had seen her attractive in the daytime would see her at night still more beautiful, although in a different way.

She always played to full houses, receiving the compliments of the cream of the Strasbourg aristocracy who would crowd into her dressing room after each performance.

One evening she was presented to a timid, serious-looking gentleman with deep-blue eyes, whose shyness contrasted sharply with his solid Alsacian build. Count François de Klinglin, the son of the chief magistrate of Strasbourg, was handsome, even if he did not have the seductive appearance of Baron D., and it was not long before Adrienne observed the certain difficulty he had in expressing himself, and surmised that the young count found her attractive. He stammered out a request for permission to pay her a visit at her house, and she graciously accorded him permission.

Flattered by his attentions, she was nonetheless too proud and knowing to encourage him. She minimized his interest, then, even while she did not refuse the distraction of allowing herself to be courted discreetly and respectfully by the young gentleman from Strasbourg with the broad shoulders and candid eyes. He would see her every day, but time passed without his ever daring to declare his love or even asking any favor of her. Nor was she in any hurry to draw him into any specific commitment, and the insecure young man would almost have been consumed by a broken heart had not an unexpected circumstance brought his suffering to a happy conclusion.

Klinglin knew he had no "right" where Adrienne was

concerned, but he could not prevent himself from being jealous. One day she informed him that she was exceedingly tired and, since she was not performing that night, she wanted to retire early. Klinglin, always haunted by the prospect of a rival bolder than himself, was quite happy with her wise decision; he left her about sundown. That night, after a late supper with friends, he was on his way home at two in the morning and could not resist the temptation to take a detour under Adrienne's window. How surprised he was, therefore, to notice the glare of a brightly lit bedroom. The young man's Alsacian blood came to a boil. Possessed with a madness he could not control, he forced the front door with one thrust of his shoulder, stealthily crossed the antechamber, bounded up the stairway in two great leaps, and burst into Adrienne's bedroom, where candles were indeed burning. But once over the threshold he remained as if transfixed, for there before him was Adrienne in her pink bed bonnet, resting on a fine lace pillow, quietly reading in her bed. Her first inclination was to scream, but at the sight of the embarrassed but happy expression on Klinglin's face, she quickly understood that there was nothing to fear. After a slight argument, Klinglin finally confessed his love and apologized for his jealousy and anger that had proved more powerful than his best intentions. She was greatly touched at his sincerity, and Klinglin did not return home until the morning.

It was perhaps on that very dawn that he committed the generous imprudence of promising marriage as soon as he became of age and thus would be free to dispose of his name. The proposal, received with tears of gratitude, was in accord with Adrienne's long-range plans. If gratitude suffices to bring on love, we must assume that from time to time this new "legitimatized" lover received a tenderness equal to those given his predecessor, Baron D.

At the beginning of the second year of their engagement, Adrienne's figure gave signs of an approaching new arrival. Unfortunately, this served as a warning to her intended groom's family who, naturally unhappy over his liaison with an actress, decided that it was time to intervene. Klinglin's father sent for him and made it quite evident that he would prefer his son to make a more advantageous marriage—one which he, Klinglin *père*, had already arranged—and added that he would answer filial disobedience with disinheritance. After a short-lived resistance, he bowed to his father's will and accepted his new fiancée.

Less than one month after Klinglin's marriage had been performed with great ceremony in Strasbourg cathedral, Adrienne gave birth to her second daughter, Françoise-Catherine-Ursule. Abandonment by her child's father marked the end of any optimistic dreams she might have held for a well-ordered life. Adrienne, once again thrown into despair, found this new shock more difficult to bear than the loss of Baron D., for this time her misfortune was complicated by the ugliness of a broken promise.

With no further desire to perform before a public who had witnessed her humiliation, she was determined to leave Strasbourg. At the end of the year 1716, she bid a definitive farewell to the provinces and left for Paris. The departure must have been cheering; not only was she preceded by her professional reputation, but she was reinforced with an order from the first gentleman of the King's chamber, directing her to choose a role for her debut at the Comédie-Française. Legrand, who had not forgotten her, had assured the Compagnie, in evocation of the memory of that great first interpreter of Racine's heroines, "I promise you a new Champmeslé."

Chapter Four

THE THEATRE ON THE
Rue Des Fossés-Saint-Germain
1717–1720

*E, STEWARD AND Controller-General of the King's silverplate, pleasures, and business of the King's chamber,* order *His Majesty's Players (in accordance with the order of Monseigneur the Duc d'Aumont, Peer of France and First Gentleman of the Chamber) to invite Mademoiselle Lecouvreur, immediately after the seasonal opening of their theatre, to perform in a play of her own choosing, in order to judge of any talent she may have for the theatre. Done in Paris this 27th day of March, 1717.*

So read the order for Adrienne's debut. At the time Paris possessed only two officially sanctioned theatres: the Royal Academy of Music (the Opéra) and the Théâtre-Français (the Comédie-Française). The Comédie-Française had been formed in 1680 and performed in Molière's old theatre on the rue Guénégaud. There was also the Comédie-Italienne, as it was called, an offshoot of the Commedia dell'Arte, which had been much more popular than the Comédie-Française. A critic of the time observed: "The general public likes a hearty laugh and this is why the Italian actors are preferred." But in 1697, the Italian players had been censured and banished after

49

the production of a play entitled *The False Prude* which was alleged to be a satire of Mme de Maintenon. Louis XIV, in response to the troupe's appeal to repeal the decree of banishment, received them coldly. In dismissing them he remarked: "You have no reason to complain that Cardinal Mazarin tempted you from Italy; you came to France on foot and you have made enough to return in your carriages." Subsequent theatres that tried to spring up on the fairgrounds of Saint-Germain were invariably closed for encroaching on the privileges of the Comédie-Française, which, in 1689, had moved from the rue Guénégaud to the new theatre built for it on the site of the Etoile tennis court in the rue des Fossés-Saint-Germain, today the rue de l'Ancienne-Comédie.

We recall that the aging Louis XIV generally avoided worldly amusements and that the courtiers and nobility followed his example for fear of losing royal favor. Of course, theatrical representations were always being given on the private stages of the Château de Chantilly, residence of the Prince de Condé, and by the Duchesse du Maine in her château at Sceaux. But even princes and princesses of the blood scarcely ventured to attend the public theatres, and when they did, it was practically in secret. The Duc d'Orléans, who spent much more time in Paris than he did with his royal uncle at Versailles, was the only exception. The public, on the other hand, exhibited a marked liking for tragedy and comedy and, in the last years of the Sun King's reign, was responsible for the continued vogue of the Comédie-Française. Still the troupe's receipts were at a minimum, and the situation did not improve until the Duc d'Orléans became Regent in 1715.

The members of the old court circle did not attend the theatre any more than they had before, but the younger courtiers were only too anxious to make up for lost time. Thus the Regency made the fortune of the theatres, which had been nearly ruined as a result of the previous reign's austerity. The Regent's court in the Palais-Royal set the fashion. Nearly every evening the Regent or members of his household, either in state or in private, attended the Opéra or the Comédie-Française. The Comédie had never been more popular.

On April 25, 1718 the Duc d'Orléans allowed the Comédie-Italienne to return. The troupe (now boasting several great actors, including Luigi Riccoboni) settled in its old theatre at the Hôtel de Bourgogne, instantly regaining the popularity it had enjoyed before its expulsion. But as the language of Goldoni was unfamiliar to the wealthy bourgeoisie without whom they could not hope to prosper, the Italians gradually resorted to plays written in French. This made the Théâtre-Italien a formidable rival of both the Opéra and the Comédie-Française.

But apart from "box office" the Comédie-Française was even then considered to be the highest expression of French dramatic art, the first theatre, not only of France, but of Europe. Its members were entitled to call themselves "Comédiens ordinaires du Roi." Like Molière's old troupe, their association had royal authorization to manage its own theatre and decided all artistic questions by a show of votes in an assembly of its members—who were *sociétaires*, or associates, each of whom shared in the profits according to a scale based on seniority and celebrity. There were 23 *parts*, or shares, which were divided among 27 *sociétaires*. Most of the 27 received either one-quarter or one-half share. The "stars" received full shares. However, in more important matters the Comédie-Française was subjected to the arbitrary authority of the first four gentlemen of the King's chamber which, until the Revolution, exercised sovereign control over the internal affairs of all the theatres of Paris. The opinions expressed by these four gentlemen were as good as law, and little could be done without their sanction. Not only did they act as arbitrators between the public and the actors, but also intervened in cases of misunderstanding between the actors themselves. They saw that regulations concerning credits and disbursements were obeyed, granted retiring pensions, sanctioned the program for each evening, sometimes reprimanded an actor who failed in his task, and—as seen above—authorized the debut of a new actor. Thus when Adrienne wished to apply for what was called the "order for her debut," she had to deal with the First Gentleman of the King's Chamber, Monseigneur le Duc d'Aumont.

The architect of the new theatre on the rue des Fossés-Saint-Germain, d'Orbay, divided the rectangular area of the old Etoile tennis court into two parts: approximately two-thirds for the audience and one-third for the stage. Spectators entered by two separate doors on the right and left, flanked by Corinthian-style columns, into the *parterre* or pit, reserved for standees. A railing separated the *parterre* from the semi-circular amphitheatre whose twenty rows of seats rose directly facing the great gilded proscenium. There were three tiers of ornate boxes along the sides, each with resplendently painted ceilings and rich hangings. Their "construction, carving, painting and gold-leaf" were, to quote an observer, "a most sparkling, rich and beautiful sight." Great chandeliers provided the only illumination; on important occasions wax candles would be substituted for the ordinary tallows. During intermissions the huge flambeaux were lowered to permit the *moucheur* to fulfill his duties—that is, to extinguish the stage candles and to replace them as need be.

The theatre could hold as many as 2,000 persons (and probably more), but the usual attendance fell far short of filling the hall. According to the *Registres* of the Comédie-Française, the largest number of paid admissions amounted to 1,586 on March 8, 1704. The smallest was when there was no performance because *"il n'est venu personne"*—no one showed up. Ordinarily, a paid attendance of 1,000 seems to have been quite satisfactory, and would have filled the theatre almost to capacity, since approximately one-third of the audience paid no admission. These privileged many included all members of the royal household (who, if they chose to attend the theatre en masse, would leave no room for paying spectators), high municipal officers, their families and secretaries, families of the actors, musketeers, and any other persons to whom the troupe felt it owed special favors.

Although the King did not attend this theatre, the Duc and Duchesse de Bourgogne did, as well as the Regent Duc d'Orléans, his mother Elisabeth-Charlotte (known popularly as the Princess-Palatine), the Duchesse de Berry, the Duchesse du Maine, the Duc de Chartres (father of Louis-Philippe), the Prince de Conti, the Duc de Vendôme, and the Duchesse de Bouillon.

The fact that Elisabeth-Charlotte, Princess-Palatine of the Rhine, Duchesse d'Orléans, and the Regent's mother, attended the theatre at all must attest to her taste for

53

spectacle rather than for any special love for the delights of Paris. Saint-Simon had referred to her as "a princess of the old school: firmly attached to honor, virtue, rank, greatness, and where proprieties were concerned, unrelenting." She was short and quite ugly, with tiny eyes, enormous nose, and great flat, hanging cheeks. In November 1672, when she had arrived in France to marry "Monsieur," the King's brother, she boasted over being "dry as a piece of wood." Her deformity appears to have come about through an attack of smallpox from which she barely recovered. Famous for her black humor, she referred to her monstrous appearance on many occasions: "I am as square as a dice." She took no care to appear delicate in manners, was full of animation, independent, and given to telling off-color jokes which caused her to give out with great bursts of laughter.

It was said that she was the best friend of her son, the Regent, whom she admired and adored. On the other hand, she abhorred the capital, finding it unclean and unhealthy and its air—even then—polluted. In December of 1715, she wrote in a letter: "It is certain that anyone who has ever seen Holland finds Germany dirty; but one has only to come to France to discover that Germany is clean, for nothing is more stinking or disgusting than Paris." Some years later, she wrote: "When I have been there just two hours my head begins to ache, I get a sore throat, and I never stop coughing."

Foreign visitors to the Comédie-Française included the King of Denmark, the Duke of Mantua, and the Turkish ambassador. When the Old Pretender, called the "Roi d'Angleterre," came to the theatre on October 18, 1706, admission charges were doubled. When the Elector of

Bavaria arrived, at first they were doubled only for places on the stage, but when he returned six days later, rates jumped throughout the house. The record does not state whether exiled royalty shared in the receipts its presence helped to increase, but prices were similarly increased when Michel Baron returned to the stage after his thirty-year retirement.

The audience was composed largely of nobles, bourgeois, and artisans. The poorer members of society could not often afford the price of admission, even to the *parterre*, though they did take advantage of free performances designed to celebrate marriages and births within the royal family, the recovery of the King or the Dauphin from illness, the making of peace, the arrival in 1722 of the Infanta, who had been betrothed to the future Louis XV. Less frequent were the benefit performances given to aid actors or their relatives. The theatre would be closed on account of great heat, or great cold, or on days of ecclesiastical feasts or services. There were also jubilees, processions, and public prayers that obliged the actors to close their doors. At times there were closings resulting from the needs of the actors themselves, as when some of them were ill or were detained by visits to the Court, by rehearsals, or other business of the troupe. At other times the theatres closed because of national spectacles, such as the reception given Peter the Great on his visit to France in 1717. (Indeed, the Czar of Russia was still in Paris the night of Adrienne's debut, May 14, 1717.)

The troupe was taxed and charged for numerous reasons, most importantly for the benefit of the poor. For this, one-sixth of their total receipts had to be deducted. A tax of a tenth of the remaining five-sixths was added, in 1716, for the benefit of the Hôtel-Dieu, the hospital for the poor. Between July of 1718 and August of 1720 the actors were allowed to subtract three hundred francs as expenses before calculating their taxes. The receipts from lower boxes, rented as units, varied from thirty to forty-five francs; from upper boxes, between fifteen to thirty. The best seats, from three and a fraction to six francs; the next best from one and a fraction to three; the *parterre*, from sixteen to twenty-five *sous*. Free performances and escalated rates all had to be considered, of course.

In 1717, twenty-seven *sociétaires* made up the Comédie-Française. Isaac-François Guérin, the *doyen* or dean, was then 82 years old and was to live for another ten years. Married to Armande Béjart, Molière's widow, his longevity allowed him to bring to the present troupe the traditions of the illustrious past.

The new *pensionnaire* was actually only a postulant at this point, since her admission to the company depended on her success. But it soon became evident to Adrienne's colleagues that Legrand had not exaggerated in promising them a new Champmeslé. Witnesses in the audience report that Adrienne was not beautiful—at least not in the usual sense of the word. "Although her face is very pleasant, a little plumpness would not be unbecoming. She is not tall but very well built and has that noble air which speaks in her favor. She is endowed with as much grace as anyone in society. Finally, the best way I could describe her would be to compare her with a miniature." Another witness reported: "Mlle Lecouvreur has neither an advantageous bearing nor many of the amenities associated with the fairer sex which charm both eyes and heart. But she is perfectly well proportioned to her average size with a noble and assured appearance, well-placed head and shoulders, fiery eyes, beautiful mouth, slightly aquiline nose, and attractive air and manner. Her cheeks are quite full, although she is not fleshy. Her features are appropriately drawn to express sadness, joy, tenderness, terror, and pity." Thus, although Adrienne was by no means beautiful, there is agreement concerning her expressiveness of movement and her possession of that elusive quality known as charm.

Of the many portraits painted of her, two are generally considered original, largely because they have served as the basis for well-known engravings: one by Drevet, *fils*, after the painting by Coypel; the other by F. G. Schmidt, after the painting by Fontaine. Our own preference is for the Drevet/Coypel engraving. Compared to the Schmidt/Fontaine engraving, there is certainly no question as to its professionalism and artistry. The other seems amateurish by comparison.[1]

One may wonder whether such an appearance would not be more fitting for a player primarily versed in comic roles. For an actress of tragedy we might very well have wished for a less pleasant appearance, but as we shall see, a "sweet" rather than "beautiful" appearance could not detract from Adrienne's ability in tragedy.

On her debut the theatre on the rue des Fossés-Saint-Germain was filled to capacity. Ensconced in tiers of boxes ringing the house and overhanging the stage were the peruked nobles in their richly brocaded suits and gilded shoes ornamented with high, red heels. With fans of painted chicken skin they cooled their rouged faces and those of their ladies in silken gowns ornamented with *blondes,* the customary delicate, lace ruffles, and hothouse roses. While members of the upper bourgeoisie also occupied the boxes, less fortunate members of this class, the tradesmen, professional people, small businessmen, and artisans, had to stand uncomfortably close together in the *parterre.*

Since this was a very special evening, the spectators in this part of the theatre, what with protecting their pockets and holding their canes, swords, cloaks, and hats —for there were no cloakrooms then—were half-suffocated by the crush and compelled to stand on tiptoe to see the actors. It was difficult to establish silence in this surging crowd. As usual, the *parterre* was surrounded by a guard of soldiers with fixed bayonets, and the officer in command had the power to arrest and eject insubordinate spectators. But the *parterre* still preserved its privilege of hissing the play or any particular actor. If its disappointment was expressed too offensively, the police, aided by the soldiers if necessary, quickly restored order. One critic wrote: "The public is irritated by the parade of armed men. . . . The theatre looks like a prison, but when the *parterre* gradually works itself up into a state of ferment, it is difficult to prevent the explosion."

On the stage itself, railed off by an iron balustrade, were four rows of cushioned seats, held as usual by the more privileged members of the aristocracy. On special occasions a fifth row of seats was placed in front of the balustrade and about fifty people were allowed to stand, ranged in a semi-circle at the back of the stage. This made matters very difficult indeed for the actors, who were very often mistaken for the spectators. When they wished to enter or leave the stage, they had to make their way through the crowd, their voices often drowned out by the hum of conversation going on around them.

The Regent and his royal guest, Peter the Great of Russia, were at the Opéra, thus leaving the great royal box vacant, but even so, this promised to be an exciting evening. Adrienne had chosen for her debut Crébillon's *Electre* and it was in the role of Orestes' sister that she would appear before the Parisian public for the first time.

The rise of the curtain did not serve to silence the chattering on stage. Indeed the nobles seated there would exchange crude jokes, engage in quarrels and even in occasional duels, deeming it a great favor to give an actor even their momentary attention.

Yet as Adrienne entered, an unusual silence fell. Free of the massive draperies and unwieldy, plumed headdress in which all actors were accustomed to appear, she wore a simple Grecian-type robe (described as "a robe *à la romaine* in white satin, trimmed in black silk-velvet") and allowed curls of her own chestnut-colored hair to fall over her bare shoulders. Not only did her costumes evoke surprise, but instead of chanting her alexandrines in the sonorous singsong customary at the time, she spoke naturally, with pauses and inflections for emphasis. Though her voice was not strong, she had an amazing range of inflection. Critics of the time did not hesitate to compare her with colleagues more advanced in age and experience.

To the critic, Adrienne appears to be the ideal and long-awaited interpreter of roles which had never been quite fulfilled by their first performers. It would appear, for instance, that training Champmeslé for *Phèdre* imposed a terrible labor upon Racine. "He taught her but with

59

much difficulty," his son, Louis, wrote. "He made her understand the lines she had to recite, showing her the movements, dictating the tones which he even notated. When he died, she was no longer the same and, as she grew older, she gave forth with great shouts which succeeded in imparting bad habits to the other actors." Even though Racine's son was obviously prejudiced against the woman who was widely known to be his father's mistress, others have agreed that Racine never was able to correct Champmeslé's singsong declamation.

But the old school of declamation had its adepts of all ages: young actresses had important support from the troupe's two tragedians *emeriti*, Mlle Desmares, the niece of Champmeslé, and Mlle Duclos, who had succeeded to the roles of Champmeslé and had been performing them for a quarter of a century. Thus, the first interpreters of Corneille and Racine—and consequently the old school of declamation—continued to reign through their direct professional descendants.

It is evident that Adrienne's acting style was considered a remarkable innovation. But her contribution to the French stage becomes even more vivid when one examines the style of her arch-rival, that relic of the old school, Mlle Duclos.

Marie-Anne de Châteauneuf Duclos, born in 1672 (and thus twenty years Adrienne's senior) had all the physical attributes one could desire in a woman of the theatre. To judge from the painting by Largillière, she was tall, imposing, well-proportioned, with two enormous eyes deeply set into a perfectly oval-shaped face. The majestic bearing in which she is portrayed went far toward making her the ideal tragic queen.

We are told, however, that Mlle Duclos was not particularly intelligent. As a matter of fact, the expression *bête comme la Duclos* (as dumb as Duclos) had become proverbial even in her own time. Voltaire reported that one of her friends once challenged: "I'll wager, Mademoiselle, that you do not know your *Credo*." "I don't know my *Credo?*" she objected, "I'll recite it for you: 'Our father which art . . .' Help me out. I don't remember the rest."

In 1719 Mlle Duclos decided to sub-lease the upper portion of her rented house on the rue des Marais to a certain Sieur Joquet d'Imonville, his wife, his wife's aunt, and a young man not related to any of them. All went well until the day when Mlle Duclos, disturbed by a loud argument coming from the sub-leased apartment, found her tenant in the process of evicting his guest, the young man, and demanding from him the repayment of a debt of 2,000 *livres*. Duclos, impressed with the youth's good looks, invited him to move into her own quarters, where she learned that he was the Chevalier de Morsan. Two days later Duclos herself repaid to Joquet d'Imonville the owed sum of 2,000 *livres*.

The new *ménage* was one of bliss. Duclos denied her young cavalier nothing, especially the jewelry and laces which were his passion. This continued for four years, until the chevalier caught smallpox and died in his benefactress' home.

The story would be quite banal up to this point were it not for certain legal proceedings instituted seven years later against the tragedienne, by means of which we learn that the Chevalier de Morsan was a woman. Her real name was Marguerite-Charlotte Donc, daughter of a Parisian notary, Charles-Henri Donc. Having been forced to marry a certain Sieur Robert at the age of 15, Marguerite-Charlotte fled the conjugal domicile disguised in man's attire. Considering his wife dead, her husband remarried. It appears that his second wife was no happier than his first and, wishing to leave him, decided to have him accused of bigamy.

To defend himself against this charge, he naturally had to prove that his first wife was dead. His investigation disclosed that his wife was indeed dead, and that Mlle Duclos had falsely declared her name to be the Chevalier de Morsan. Priests, neighbors, servants were called as witnesses and, after seven years, the body never having been exhumed, the matter was dropped, not without great amusement and frivolity on the part of a public which had concluded that Duclos had a preference for women.

Even so, her beauty had won her important protectors. Voltaire was among her adorers in his very early years. But her preference for the Duc d'Uzès caused Voltaire to write:

> My heart was for a time charmed by la Duclos
> Cupid had set my lyre in her direction;
> I sang the praises of la Duclos;
> D'Uzès got the good of them—
> I should not even have bothered!

Less poetically he wrote: "Every morning Mlle Duclos takes several doses of Senna, and in the evening, several doses of d'Uzès." The latter medicine seemed to do her the most good! D'Uzès and other highly-placed contacts made it possible for her to be engaged at the Opéra, where her talent was less than mediocre, and later at the Comédie-Française, where the power and tonality of her musical voice made her reputation. She was soon the acclaimed principal actress of the company. But only too aware of the vocal advantage she held over her colleagues, she abused her gift to the extreme. Eventually she no longer recited her roles, but instead intoned them in exaggerated cadence.

According to Voltaire, who attempted to trace the history of this taste for chanted declamation, it evolved naturally from the *mélopée*, or chanted chorus which Aristotle in his *Poetics* had deemed essential to tragedy. In the sixteenth century, the Italian revival of tragedy as a *genre* made use of the *mélopée*, and the French borrowed this usage from the Italians.

It was, after all, the continuation of a long tradition bequeathed by the greats of the past, and the public did have a taste for it. If we bear in mind that eloquent tirades and declarations of love in the *précieux* style are not at all rare in French tragedy, then we must excuse France's first tragedians for having intoned the tirades and sighed the declarations. The actors were simply inspired by the style in which they had been written. The farewell of Berenice, for example, easily lends itself to incantation:

> ⚜ *Je n'écoute plus rien: et, pour jamais,*
> *adieu . . .*
> *Pour jamais! Ah, Seigneur! songez-vous en*
> *vous-même*
> *Combien ce mot cruel est affreux quand on*
> *aime?*
> *Dans un mois, dans un an, comment*
> *souffrirons-nous,*

63

Seigneur, que tant de mers me séparent
de vous;
Que le jour recommence, et que le jour finisse
Sans que jamais Titus puisse voir
Bérénice. . . .

I listen no more: and, forever, goodbye . . .
Forever! Ah, My Lord, reflect
How atrocious that cruel word is when one
loves
In a month, in a year, how will we allow
My Lord, so many seas to separate me from
you;
And the day to begin and end
With Titus powerless to glimpse
Berenice . . .

The tonality of these lines could demand or even force a musical intonation.

Voltaire approved this type of chant so long as it supported the performance of actors who were "ingenious and sensitive." When used by a less masterly actor, however, its effect was nothing more than ridiculous:

> *Mélopée théâtrale* perished with the actress
> Duclos who possessed only a beautiful voice
> without soul and wit and who finally rendered
> ridiculous what had been so admired in the
> actresses Des Oeillets and Champmeslé.

Mlle Duclos played all her roles alike, giving little evidence of having studied her characters in depth. Since there were no gestures or facial expressions which might bring lucidity to a given situation, one must have had great difficulty in distinguishing her Hermione from her Phèdre. But knowing that she was in fashion, admired, discussed, Duclos had little reason to change her method. When Adrienne Lecouvreur was called upon to share with Duclos the roles of tragic princess and queen, it was, of course, too late for the older actress to change her style.

Duclos, then, by means of the strained effects of her voice, strove to transmit to the audience the harmony of her lines. Adrienne, by speaking her lines as she understood their meaning, and by attempting to lend to each word its just weight, sought to interpret Voltaire's thought. Her poses appeared more natural, less stilted, and less automatic. Lastly, Adrienne knew how to listen, her face reflecting the feelings of the actor who was speaking. To the public of the 1720s this was truly a reform in itself. The illustrious *Mercure de France* summed up Adrienne's contribution to acting in this way: "To her belongs the glory of having introduced simple, noble, and natural declamation and banishing cant." It should be noted that in matters of the theatre the *Mercure* was considered the best, if not the only, authority. But to protect its income, its editors had to take care not to injure readers with criticism that might be considered too sharp, pointed, or direct.

Luigi Riccoboni, known as Lélio, the leading player of the Comédie-Italienne and Marivaux's favorite actor, had no such problems. Shocked by the way his colleagues of the Comédie-Française would expend their energy in loud and needless outbursts of voice, he wrote in his didactic poem on stage technique:

> *La leggiadra Couvreur sola non trotta*
> *Per quella strada dove i suoi compagni,*
> *Ven di galoppo tutti quanti en frotta,*

Se aviene ch'ella piangia, o che se lagni
Senza quegli urli spaventèvoli loro,
Ti muove si che in pianger l'accompagni,
E piace mi in sentire, che a coloro
Che il declamare adorano pur piace,
E con gli altri in lodarla fanno coro

⚜ Only charming Lecouvreur does not travel
The road upon which all her colleagues
Trot at an unbridled pace;
If she should cry or implore,
Without frightening you to death as they do
   with their howling
She is so touching that you are obliged to feel
Her sorrow and are amazed to see that
Even the staunchest partisans of declamation
Join in her praises.

The same idea was conveyed by one of Adrienne's admirers who wrote in an *Epître:*

⚜ *Enfin le vrai triomphe, et la fureur tragique*
Fait place sur la scène au tendre, au pathétique.

⚜ At last reality triumphs, and tragic madness
Gives up the stage to sensitivity, to the deeply
   moving.

Similarly, in lines written to be placed under the bust of Adrienne as she appears in the Drevet engraving, another has our heroine say:

⚜ *Le théâtre me doit cet heureux changement*
Qui d'un chant déplacé proscrivit l'imposture.
La première je suis, fidèle à la nature,
Par le geste et la voix peindre le sentiment.
Pour Camille en fureur, pour Monime trompée
Que n'eut, en me voyant, laissé couler des
   pleurs.

⚜ The theatre is indebted to me for the fortunate
change
Which banished the trickery of an unneeded
song.
Faithful to nature, I am the first
To depict feeling through movement and
voice.
Seeing me as Camille gone mad or Monime
deceived.
Who would not shed tears?

In her tragic roles, Adrienne's dominant qualities won
great admiration from the critics:

> This inimitable actress had the admirable
> appearance of penetrating herself to the point
> necessary in order to express the great passions
> and to make them felt in all their strength. First
> she would go to the heart and keenly strike it
> with an intelligence, soundness, and skill which
> are impossible to describe. In almost all the great
> tragic roles, never has pathos been pushed as far.

Thus, when Adrienne arrived at the Comédie-Française, she encountered the pitiless shouting which had
been passed down by the adored actresses of the past. In
a short time, however, and in spite of the stubborn opposition of her rivals, Adrienne was able to bring on a
veritable revolution, which could never have taken place
without the immediate approval of the public. Shouted
cant was to give way to nuanced diction; melody was
to give way to harmony.

At a time when the art of speaking was an enviable and
treasured asset, less fortunate magistrates and churchmen
did not hesitate to seek out good actors to help them
perfect whatever speaking ability they may have had.

67

The Marquis de la Chalotais, Procurer-General of the Parlement of Brittany and longtime friend of Adrienne, wrote to her of his disappointment at not being in Paris where he could benefit from her coaching. We are indebted to him for thus providing the only occasion in Adrienne's correspondence where she not only referred to her own acting, but defined it:

> You say that you would like me to teach you the art of declamation which you need. Have you forgotten that I do not declaim at all? My acting's simplicity is its only—if weak—merit; but this simplicity which chance has fashioned successfully in me, seems to me to be indispensable to a man like you. First one needs as much intelligence as you have, and then let nature do the rest. To wish to exaggerate nature is to lose her. Grace, nobility, and simplicity in expression, giving force only to reasoning and to objects— this is what you will say and do better than anyone.

Adrienne's natural manner may have been a direct result of her delicate physical means. In spite of its qualities of depth and tone, her voice lacked strength. But she strove to overcome this shortcoming:

> Although she is slight of voice, she pleased the public from the first and continues to please, because it finds . . . her acting . . . all the more pleasant in that she studied how to handle it and to proportionate it to her own strength; and thus one might say that her lack of lung power contributed this measure of perfection.

Adrienne's diction was considered perfect, an honor attributed both to her own good taste and to the coaching she was given by the grammarian-philosopher César Chesneau Du Marsais (1676–1756). This author of a treatise on logic, who later became the *Encyclopédie*'s expert in questions of grammar, was an excellent analyst of the natural laws of language. A nineteenth-century critic was to write that Du Marsais was to the eighteenth century what Vaugelas and the Gentlemen of Port-Royal had been to the seventeenth.

Adrienne and Du Marsais met on the evening of her debut in Paris. It was he—or so the story goes—who could be heard commenting to himself in a low voice "*Bon, cela!*" (that was good) each time the actress had executed a tirade, line, or word in a manner which pleased him. Adrienne, curious to know why her performance at certain points was judged better by the gentleman in the box, whose enthusiasm appeared slightly more than moderate, sent him a note inviting him to meet with her privately. Du Marsais is said to have asked Adrienne to recite a passage of her choosing. She graciously obliged, managing to obtain only two or three "*Bon, cela!*" for her trouble. Greatly embarrassed, she asked for an explanation. Du Marsais replied: "Mademoiselle, it is my opinion that never has an actress given more reason to hope for more talent than yours, and if you wish to go far beyond any actress before you, I dare guarantee that all you need do is give to words the just value required for what they must express." She followed the advice of her guest, who consented to coach her in diction. Their relationship developed into enduring friendship. In her correspondence she invariably referred to Du Marsais as the *philosophe*.

Adrienne performed 139 times in her opening season of 1717–18, an extraordinary number for a beginner. In fact, she herself would come close to this figure only once, when she performed 135 times in the 1722–23 season. The smallest number of performances she gave was 50 in 1724–25, due to certain personal circumstances which we shall investigate later on.

But that first season her most popular roles were that of Pulchérie, daughter of a dethroned emperor of Constantinople, in Corneille's *Héraclius*, an enormously complicated melodrama of generosity and self-denial; Monime in Racine's tragedy of senile passion *Mithridate* (her third most popular role throughout her career after Racine's *Iphigénie* and Houdard de la Motte's *Ines de Castro*); Alcmène—her one really successful comic role—in Molière's idealization of Louis XIV's court, *Amphitryon;* and Zénobie in that murder-thriller, *Rhadamiste et Zénobie* by Jolyot de Crébillon, written in the worst taste of the period. Its author once remarked: "Corneille has taken heaven, Racine the earth, hell is left for me."

Du Marsais' suggestions brought obvious results. A critic later observed: "Her manner of reciting proved that she applied herself to what she was saying and understood it perfectly." Another pointed out: "She had, in the highest degree, what is called guts and feeling: she understood perfectly the sense of the words she was reciting." As a necessary consequence, gesture was made to agree with correctness of deliverance. We learn from various witnesses that "her eyes spoke as much as her mouth and often made up for her lack of voice." "Per-

70

haps never has the art of silences been so well understood, that is to say, the sense of what the actor onstage
with her was saying, so well understood and so well expressed." "She gave her arms inimitable charm, her eyes
announced what she was about to say." "She treated perfectly all details of a role and thus made one forget the
actress; all one saw was the character she portrayed."
Thus the interpreter was subordinated to the poet's creation.

Critics did not always rationalize Adrienne's lack of
physical strength, seeing in it a reason for her great talent.
Indeed, they often defined her talent by means of that
limitation. We recall that Adrienne was once compared
to a miniature. In the same article we find ". . . thus we
do not find in her those thrusts of strength which im-
press and which, so to speak, force the admiration of
connoisseurs." Or, as put by another critic: "She excelled
in those roles where finesse rather than strength was
needed." This may explain Adrienne's lack of talent or
even interest in low comedy roles. The *Mercure de
France*, having just finished extolling her qualities as a
tragedian, did not hide its observations concerning her
talent in the comic *genre:* "In comedy she played and
was successful only in a small number of roles." On many
occasions she performed Alcmène, of course, but in
Amphitryon we have a heroic comedy which often re-
quires the tragic tone. However, as Célimène in the same
author's *Misanthrope*, a role considered to be the touch-
stone of the coquette, it would appear that she barely
tried out. In thirteen years, she appeared in this role only
nine times, playing Elmire in *Tartuffe* only four times.

To complete the record, we are obliged to say that

on one important occasion she failed dismally. Marivaux, then the rage of the Comédie-Italienne, decided to try his art at the Comédie-Française, offering his *Seconde Surprise de l'Amour* to the troupe and choosing Adrienne to play the principal role, that of the Marquise. It was reported that she was "affected and mannered" and that she performed the role of a marquise "as though she were playing a queen." That is to say, she played a fanciful character with an excessive solemnity.

But this regal bearing was inseparable from Adrienne's acting. According to the *Mercure*, the audience had seen "a princess who was playing comedy for her own pleasure." It would appear that at times this quality served her well: "She has that marvelous weakness of allowing the role to overtake her, and in so doing she mistook false for true, thus communicating her own pleasure to the audience so that it too was pleased by the sweet charm of its own deception." For some, this was a dangerous quality: "She was often out of sorts. Her acting was not convincing unless she was moved by a role that pleased her or by some interesting object." *

In April 1720, three years after her Parisian debut, Michel Baron came to give Adrienne the support of his name, talent, and time-defying vigor. The celebrated actor, a glorious ghost of the heroic age, a comrade and pupil of Molière, came out of a thirty-year retirement at the age of 67 to join with a talent he considered similar to his own. The two entered into a continuing relation-

---

* Later in the century, Mlle Clairon would be Diderot's model for his *Paradox of the Actor* in which he praised her total impassivity vis-a-vis her roles. It was said that during her most impassioned scenes she could and would mentally review her household accounts.

ship which found them starring opposite one another until the end of their lives (they were to die only seven months apart), and were soon to be generally considered the leading actor and actress of France.

Molière had taken great pleasure in forming Baron's supple talent in a *genre* in which Molière himself had but mediocre ability. Unhappy with previous actors' attempts at interpreting the ideas dear to his heart, Molière saw in Baron's art the personification of those concepts set forth in the *Impromptu de Versailles:* the question of *naturel* and *vérité* in acting. Unlike his rivals in the troupe of the Hôtel de Bourgogne, Molière insisted that the actor recite "as naturally as possible, humanly," because "a king who is conversing alone with his captain of the guard would hardly take on a demoniacal air." Molière imposed this manner of acting on all his actors, but after his death, when the actors of the Troupe de Molière joined with his old rivals at the Hôtel de Bourgogne—and especially after Baron's first retirement—this doctrine had to be abandoned. Thus the style of playing for obvious and easy effect, of gaining applause by means of momentary displays of *coups de gueule* became the criteria of success.

Adrienne had already assured the victory of her revolution. Now, with the added support of Baron and the continuing acclaim of the public, one might suppose that her side had won. In the theatre, as in all institutions, however, there is a constant struggle between tradition and progress, each in turn victorious but hardly ever reconciled.

Another of Adrienne's innovations, of course, was the desire for authenticity in costume. As Elisabeth in Thomas

Corneille's *Le Comte d'Essex*, she gave up, once and for all, the pompous and heavy robes that her colleagues would apply indifferently to Grecian, Roman, and modern periods, appearing instead in the attire of the English court. The lavishness of her wardrobe is fully attested to in the posthumous inventory of her belongings; Mlle Pellissier of the Opéra would later pay the sum of 40,000 *livres* for Adrienne's wardrobe. It included twelve *habits à la Romaine*, that is, dresses in the ancient style or so thought to be. Two were in white damask, two in fire-colored velvet, two in crimson velvet, one in black damask, two in white satin (one of which was ascertained to be the costume Adrienne had worn as Electre). In the inventory, each dress is described in detail. For example:

> *Item:* an *habit à la Romaine* in cherry velvet, with train embroidered in Spanish point with hanging tufts and silver fringe; velvet skirt embroidered in silver Spanish point; silver fringe on the shoulder knots.

There was also a court dress in dark blue damask. Four *habits à la Française*, for the modern repertory, included two in cherry-colored *moiré*, one in light grey damask, and one in white muslin. Several of these robes were valued as high as 1,000 *livres* apiece. It would appear that Adrienne had a marked repugnance for one particular costume. She was once "fined six *livres* for not donning her robe for the ceremony scene of the *Malade Imaginaire*," and the registers show that she was fined the maximum amount for the same infraction each time the ceremony scene was to be performed.

To judge the strong influence these innovations had

upon future generations of actresses in the Comédie-Française, we may compare Adrienne's inventory with that of the great actress of the nineteenth century, Rachel, in which is found a listing of costumes made of simple woolens, soberly embroidered in silver and gold. The actor Talma had instituted this reform on the advice of the painter, Jacques Louis David. David was aware of only one aspect of ancient costume; but judging from the relatively stark classical statues and bas-reliefs that were being uncovered at the close of the eighteenth century, the intellectuals thus assumed that ancient dress was simpler than it actually was. Today we know that the ancients indeed loved rich clothing and showy ornaments, and this knowledge has resulted in present-day costumes being much closer to the style adopted by Adrienne Lecouvreur.

Adrienne's jewels were given a value of 4,827 *livres.* Among them are listed:

> Bracelet containing 10 diamonds, 8 small emeralds, and 1 topaz, attached to six strands of small pearls.
>
> Bracelet containing 17 small, fine brilliants.
>
> Pair of pendant earrings containing six large diamonds, 28 small diamonds, and hanging pearl clusters.
>
> Necklace of 16 pearl strands, garnished with 28 brilliants.

Now the current rage, holding a privileged place in the public's esteem, Adrienne Lecouvreur was in a position to choose her authors from among the many who presented their plays to the troupe for consideration. Naturally, those who became "her" authors also became her close friends. Voltaire is the most famous of those who admired her without reserve after their plays achieved some measure of success through her art. But there were others, whose defective playwriting was more than good acting could redeem, who lost no. time in holding Adrienne responsible for their lack of success. Although the Church was hardly friendly toward the theatre, a number of abbés were not so eager to maintain their distance from it, and a certain Abbé Nadal managed to concoct a badly written tragedy *Antiochus, ou les Macchabées* which had only seven performances. In the preface to its published version he praised Mlle Duclos in glowing terms (she had played the role of Salomé), and did not even mention Adrienne, who had played Zoraide. Voltaire immediately aimed his sharpest arrows at the unfortunate Nadal for having "accused Mlle Lecouvreur for having performed badly one time in her life and thus making it impossible for the Abbé to be applauded one time in his."

Chapter Five

ADRIENNE IN
Society

CTORS OF THE period were victims of injustice and prejudice. Considered inferior human beings, they were automatically excommunicated by the Church under a ban which had been pronounced by early councils sitting in Gaul, and the Gallican Church of the Bourbons jealously adhered to all their enactments as an assertion of its independence of Rome. Excluded by society, actors were also obliged to submit to any humiliation or insult the public might inflict upon them while they were on stage. If they dared resent publicly the insults levelled against them, they were often hauled off to prison where they were confined until they apologized to those who had injured them. The prison of For-l'Evêque was reserved especially for recalcitrant actors and actresses. Jean-Jacques Rousseau wrote that in all countries actors were despised and their profession was considered disgraceful. Although he had no wish to condemn a profession which he loved and esteemed, Diderot could not refrain from attributing to it "a shadow of contempt."

The eighteenth-century actor had succeeded, however, in advancing one step beyond his seventeenth-century counterpart: he no longer lived totally apart from society.

Now he was received in the salons, into literary circles, and private homes. Under Louis XIV, the actors Lagrange and Floridor, both of irreproachable reputation, had never been accorded such honors. Madame d'Epinay tells us that she would often dine at the home of Mlle Quinault. But despite this apparent elevation of social status, society had not at all changed its attitude toward either the actor or acting profession. In her *Mémoires* Madame d'Epinay was careful to write that she attended Mlle Quinault's suppers only to appease Mme de Jully, who had insisted that Mme d'Epinay accompany her to "that lovely debauchery."

The Maréchal de Richelieu, as fond as he was of Mlle Clairon, allowed her to be imprisoned in For-l'Evêque on April 15, 1765: she had refused to perform one evening in order to show her annoyance at what she considered to be an insult to her profession. It should be noted, however, that her progress to For-l'Evêque was a triumphal procession and all fashionable Paris flocked to visit her. To the police officer who was to take her to prison, she declaimed: "I submit to the King's orders. Everything I have is at His Majesty's disposal—my property, my person, my life. But my honor must remain intact. The King himself has no claim on that." "Of course," the officer replied, "where there is nothing, the King loses his rights."

The doors of the salons were indeed open to certain actors, but their function at these gatherings was strictly to amuse. Objects of curiosity, they were accepted as some sort of spiritual parasite, and at times their hosts did not hesitate to remind them of this. Michel Baron himself, attempting to return one afternoon to the home of his noble mistress in the midst of a grand reception, was refused entrance. Having forced his way into the great salon, he was faced by the outraged hostess who had been in his arms the night before. When she asked why he had come uninvited, he replied in an equally cold manner, "Madame, I left my bed cap behind."

Actors and actresses thus remained on the margin of society. Applauded, flattered, sought after as companions in debauchery, they were nonetheless forbidden access into a world which victimized them for a way of life it forced upon them. For Adrienne Lecouvreur, however, exceptions were made.

Her refined manner, her dependable and discreet nature were quickly recognized. Although it is almost devoid of references to her professional life, her correspondence reveals the extent of her social connections. Aside from Du Marsais, d'Argental, and Maurice de Saxe, we find the often-repeated names of the Marquis de Rochemore, the Duc de Richelieu, the Comte de Caylus, the Comte de Belle-Isle, the Chevalier de Beringhen, the Maréchal de Bezons, the Marquis de la Chalotais, the Duc de Gesvres, the Abbé d'Amfreville, Foncemagne, Piron, Fontenelle, and Voltaire. Among her close, personal friends she counted such illustrious women as the Duchesse du Maine, the Duchesse de Gesvres, the Marquise de Simiane (granddaughter and publisher of Mme de Sévigné), Mme de Pomponne, Mme de Montchesne, Mme de Fontaine-Martel, and the Présidente Berthier. The Marquise de Lambert, whose own salon gave a mark of distinctive integrity to anyone invited, doubly honored Adrienne by inviting her twice each week, to her "Tuesdays" for the fashionable aristocracy, and her "Wednesdays" reserved for professional people and intellects. She also once invited Adrienne to spend an entire week at her country estate at Clamart.

For Adrienne these relationships were not at all superficial; indeed, an important part of her day was given over to arranging for the traditional after-theatre supper. Although she preferred to receive supper guests after an exhausting performance, she very often would be forced to accept an unwanted invitation. On such occasions she would perform her worldly duties "although tired and very weak" and would often attend in her dressing gown. For her own suppers, she arranged for groups of friends who, by reason of similar interests, would enjoy being together. Custom dictated that for a given occasion she call upon a friend considered to be the most qualified and ask him to *nommer*—that is, make a list of guests: "Let me know which day you would like to have supper at my house. I shall see to it that whomever you care to invite is there, since I am well assured that you could not choose wrongly."

A well-known observer of the day stated that Adrienne Lecouvreur and Michel Baron actually initiated the custom of reciting at private gatherings: "Mlle Lecouvreur, who was extremely sought after in the best houses of Paris as well as at the Court, would not refuse to recite for such company several beautiful passages as well as entire scenes from the tragedies, to the enchantment of the other guests; it was very rare indeed for persons of her profession to recite outside of the theatre."

The demands of both professional and social life inevitably resulted in acute fatigue. But professional success could come only at the price of a dutiful social life. Adrienne bore these duties with resignation: "The forced, dismal dissipation in which I find myself is a horrible thing: trips to Versailles, the failure of new productions

80

to which one gave so much time and energy, the depression my friends have caused me for some time together with that unbearable fatigue." In a charming letter to Maurice de Saxe, Adrienne fully described how she was victimized by such demands:

> I spend my days doing at least three-quarters
> of what I find distasteful: meeting new people
> (which is impossible to avoid if I wish to
> maintain my connections) preventing me from
> devoting myself to old friends or from simply
> busying myself at home . . . It has become an
> established fashion to dine or have supper with
> me because several duchesses have done me this
> honor. There are people whose goodness and
> kindness delight and satisfy, but to whom I
> cannot devote myself because I am owned by the
> public and am absolutely forced to respond to
> every lady who might take a fancy to meet me.
> If I do not, I am accused of impertinence. It
> seems that no matter how careful I am, I am
> constantly causing dissatisfaction. If, because
> of my poor health—which as you know is quite
> weak—I must refuse an invitation or be absent
> from a gathering of ladies whom I probably have
> never seen and whose interest in me is only out of
> curiosity or . . . out of a desire to be
> fashionable, . . . one of the ladies might say:
> "Really! Isn't she playing the grand lady!"
> Another adds: "That's because we are not titled!"
> If I attempt to be serious, since one cannot be
> very gay with most people one does not know:
> "Is she that girl with so much wit?" exclaims
> one of the company. "Isn't it obvious that she's
> turning her nose up at us," says another, and
> "one must know Greek in order to satisfy her."

81

"She is a member of Mme de Lambert's circle,"
says another, "doesn't that solve the riddle for
you?" . . . I could go on at length telling of
these evil remarks. Their effect has been to give
me more than ever the desire to be free, no longer
having to court anyone except those who are kind
to me and who solace both my mind and heart.
My vanity does not require great numbers to
compensate for the true merit of the individual;
I have no desire to be brilliant; I have one hundred
times more pleasure in being silent and listening
to good things in a pleasant group of wise and
virtuous people, than to be made numb by all
the insipid praises that are lavished on me without
rime or reason in many places. It is not that I
lack gratitude or the desire to please, but I find
that the approbation of fools is only superficially
pleasant, and that it becomes a burden when it
has to be bought with continued special favors.

Adrienne expressed this same sensitivity in many other
letters: "I have always believed truth and candor to be
powerful resources; I have felt all the better for it my
whole life. I think that one must use them in everything;
it is a sure way to gain respect even for one's shortcom-
ings." And further: "The esteem of decent people is the
greatest good I know."

The luxurious trappings and sumptuous surroundings
of her house on the rue des Marais were the perfect setting
for the longed-for private life limited to a small circle of
intimate friends and illustrious personalities.[2]

One entered the courtyard from the street through the
great vaulted doorway. Carriage house, stable, and kitchen
were close to the entrance. Ascending the ornate,
wrought-iron stairway at the end of the courtyard, one

crossed an antechamber, then a passageway used as a large wardrobe. Pulling aside a heavy tapestry portiere revealed the door to Adrienne's bedroom. Six Flanders tapestries depicting tiny people scattered amidst vast areas of greenery overhung a wall covering of crimson damask. Above the fireplace was a double *trumeau* mirror over which was draped a tapestry of gamboling cupids. The mantelpiece was dominated by a great Boucherat clock, its gold-plated figures continuing the cupid motif. The fireplace opening, hidden by a small, white satin screen, was flanked by two deep and overstuffed chairs, upholstered in gold- and silver-specked silk with green damask border. Opposite the fireplace, a spinette, painted in Chinese figures. A *chaise-longue*, upholstered in a tapestry of Chinese figures, was hidden behind a six-paneled screen.

A heavily canopied and draped four-poster facing the high windows was covered with a luxurious foot-quilt decorated in small red bouquets on a white background and lined in lemon taffeta. One of the doors of the ornate *armoire* was mirrored. A silver candle holder shared a gold-leafed console with two fine porcelain vases and a pair of silk eye-blinds. Two *canapés*, one in green damask, the other in black Morocco, complete the furnishings.

The dominant colors of this intimate sanctuary of Adrienne Lecouvreur were red and green, well contrived to be representative of the moods of the mistress of the house, or at any rate, of the moods she wished to convey. When a few intimates were invited from time to time, they were more often friends than lovers. Here we imagine Du Marsais, Rochemore, d'Argental, and Voltaire, seated in a semicircle, regaling Adrienne with news and wit as she reclined on her *chaise-longue* wearing one of

83

her many dressing gowns, perhaps the one in olive-colored silk, lined in striped taffeta and speckled with a network of silver thread.

It is on the floor above that her books were kept. Adrienne, who owned priceless jewels and a sumptuous collection of silver plate (from which she once realized a fortune in order to assist Maurice de Saxe in his Courland expedition), did not possess what may be called a library. The several hundred volumes appear to have come to Adrienne by chance rather than by design. According to the inventory made after her death, they were stacked into two piles in separate closets. Their titles give no hint of any reasoned preference in choice: Bayle's *Dictionary* next to a history of France by Father Daniel; the *Revolutions of England* by Father d'Orléans. We do find the works of Rabelais as well as the *Fables* of La Fontaine, both works magnificently bound, doubtlessly the gifts of some generous admirer. But there were also works whose inconsequential nature confirms our original impression: the poetry of Mme Deshoulières, the *Histoire d'Alfarache*, one of Lesage's mediocre novels, the *Comptes Faits* of Barême, the letters of Mme Desnoyers, the *Mémoires* of Sully and of Mme de Motteville. Especially noteworthy is the lack of works dealing with the theatrical profession. The works of Racine and several unbound plays by other authors are mentioned, but Corneille was conspicuously not represented and, according to the bookseller who made the inventory, the rest of the collection was not worth the effort to catalog.

Adrienne was never able to enjoy fully the pleasures that privacy brings. Her wavering health brought on long periods of depression. Her friends often bore the brunt of her *papillons noirs,* and this added to her suffering: "I cannot bring myself to master the moods which too often afflict me. This is a fault common to my sex, and one we do not often have the good will to admit. In the end I suffer more from these moods than do the others. Since I am the first to be aware of them, I am at once precipitated into nightmarish thoughts." At times, however, this melancholy operated as a kind of dark pleasure: "I spent the entire day at home suffering. But this was not totally unbearable since my discomfort gave rise to pleasant thoughts. You are not familiar with this state of mind because you are neither weak, nor melancholy, nor a woman."

Adrienne had no taste for gossip, either professional or social, and matters of this sort thus took up little space in her correspondence. Only once, and then at the insistence of d'Argental who was then in London, did she pass on stories of the goings-on in Paris and at Versailles without the slightest shadow of wicked intent. One passage concerns the Duc de Bourbon, known for his thrifty ways: "Monsieur le Duc is getting married. He's calling for his bride in four old carriages. They say that he's giving her four new dresses, two dozen blouses, and several *blondes.*" The word *blonde* was the name given to a detachable lace ruffle worn down the front of a lady's blouse. The implication, of course, was that the Duc de Bourbon sought to economize by buying his future wife as few dresses as possible to be worn with various blouses and lace ruffles to give the impression that she had a large wardrobe.

Apparently Adrienne felt quite keenly the disadvantages of being a woman, chiefly because emotional honesty seemed to be a masculine prerogative: "Like love, friendship too has its enthusiasts. I am a member of a sex and of a profession in which men do not eagerly seek after this noble sentiment. And friendship is the only flattery I desire. I feel myself worthy of it by virtue of the manner in which I feel it and in which I have more than once inspired it." Not only did she set forth her feelings on friendship, but she listed the steps necessary to embrace it. What a far cry from Mlle de Scudéry's *Carte de tendre* of a century earlier!

> My heart suffices in all things. I listen to it and then act, and I have always been the better for it. Take me as I am or leave me. I use all my resources to prevent myself from jumping headstrong into whatever emotion I may have. First, I seek integrity, even in my weakest relationships. When kindness is joined to integrity, I know how to appreciate it, nature having provided me with a wonderful instinct for recognizing it. Social custom, the times in which we live, and a small amount of reason, have convinced me that tolerance is in great demand. Those who need no indulgence lose nothing where I am concerned. In place of it I give them the respect and admiration they deserve; and if they honor me with a few kindnesses, you may well imagine what gratitude can add to such feelings. And assuredly, I have never been ungrateful.

Once she had achieved a friendship, there was no room for negligence. Demands must come from both parties: "When, after having given the matter much thought, I adopt someone into the circle of those I love, I will not be neglected nor will I neglect. In this life, once people value each other's friendship, they must see each other. Life is all too short, but more so for those of us who have already lived." If she were ill, she would not tolerate a friend's not asking news of her, nor would she look fondly upon one who, having left for a trip, had not visited her before the departure. Thus understood, friendship must continue into old age: "It seems to me that not to be with one's friends is not to live, and that life is too short to waste its one real pleasure. As we get older we must redouble our zeal, respect, confidence, and presence."

Because of the length of their relationship, Voltaire must be placed first among her friends. They first met during the 1719–20 season when Adrienne was performing the title role in his ill-fated *Artémire*, which was withdrawn after eight representations. It would appear that the young author was not easily able to duplicate the striking success he had made the previous season: at the age of twenty-four, after a short stay at the Bastille (where he had been imprisoned in 1718 after an accusation of having composed verses insulting to the Regent), his *Oedipe* had made him famous.

After a stay in Holland, which for him exemplified all that was politically and socially liberal in the eighteenth century, Voltaire was to return to Paris in 1724 with a new version of *Artémire* entitled *Mariamne* with Adrienne in the principal role and Michel Baron as Hérode. Alas, it enjoyed even less success than before. At the moment when Mariamne, who had been condemned to drink a potion of poison, lifted the cup to her lips, someone in the *parterre* cried out: "Look, the Queen drinks!" (The rough equivalent of our modern "Cheers!") This caused such merriment among the spectators that the play could not be continued.

The records show only that single performance. Voltaire decided to give it yet another try, and the following season, on April 10, 1725, the Comédie-Française presented it in its third and definitive form entitled *Hérode et Mariamne,* with indeed what must have been considered an all-star cast: Adrienne as Mariamne, Michel Baron as Hérode, and Mlle Duclos as Salomé. This particular representation will be discussed in the following chapter.

It is supposedly during a performance of this play in December of 1725 that the famous incident between Voltaire and the Chevalier de Rohan-Chabot had its beginnings. It was generally known that François Arouet, the son of a bourgeois notary, began calling himself Arouet de Voltaire once his notoriety began to take hold. Known for his jibes and cutting wit, he thus made himself vulnerable to the disparaging remarks of those who pretended to resent his taking on a noble-sounding name —a fashion among the bourgeoisie and, as we have seen, also among actors and actresses. The second son of the Duc de Rohan-Chabot, noticing Arouet several boxes from him during the performance, made no attempt to whisper: "Who is that young man with such a loud voice?"

Voltaire, not about to ignore an occasion for a deserved witticism, replied: "He is a man who does not drag a great name through the mud, but one who knows how to honor the one he does bear." The Chevalier raised his cane, remarking that this is how one should reply. Voltaire quickly drew his sword, and Adrienne, noticing the entire incident from the stage, quickly fainted.

This ended the matter for the moment, but three days later the Chevalier had Voltaire soundly beaten by two of his lackeys. Voltaire's highly-placed friends turned their backs on him, and when the Chevalier saw that he had the upper hand, he lost no time in having the play-wright arrested and put into the Bastille. After an intern-ment of one month—and as a condition for his release—Voltaire *chose* to go to England, where he was to remain until 1729. Those seeking to prove that Voltaire was Adrienne's lover have quoted his letter to Thierot (writ-ten when Adrienne had already been dead for a year) in which he stated that he had been her *admirateur, ami, amant.* Assuming that the final word had already taken on its present-day meaning of a man who receives the favors of a woman to whom he is not married, we must conclude that Voltaire, carried away by the sentiment of the mo-ment, and secure in the knowledge that he could not be contradicted, took poetic license. It would be fairer to Voltaire if we assumed that he used the word *amant* in its older meaning—one who loves a woman openly and who may or may not be loved in return. If so, this would clearly explain all the other references to their relation-ship made by Voltaire during Adrienne's lifetime. For example, he once wrote her:

> Be the fortune of one and the desire of everyone
> And may your loves equal the duration
> Of the poor friendship my heart has for you.

We know the identity of this unique recipient of the "fortune desired by everyone," and it certainly was never Voltaire. We can be sure, in any case, that Adrienne had the good sense to turn Voltaire into a friend, but equally, there can be no doubt that he was an unhappy lover. Along with a gift of a coverlet for her bed, Voltaire could not resist sending the following note:

⚜ *Recevez dans vos bras mes illustres rivaux:*
C'est un mal nécessaire et je vous le pardonne;
Mais songez que chez vous j'ai gardé les
manteaux,
Et que c'est moi qui vous en donne.

⚜ Receive in your arms my illustrious rivals:
It is a necessary evil for which I forgive you;
But remember that in your house I wore a
disguise,
And that it is I who deceive you.

Adrienne's apparent rejection of Voltaire as a lover was accepted by him almost immediately. The curious poem entitled *Anti-Giton*, which had originally been dedicated to the actress Duclos but which Voltaire later rededicated to Adrienne, has been quoted in part by most of Adrienne's biographers who appear to favor its opening lines:

> Oh sweet sovereign of the stage,
> Beautiful Chloe, daughter of Melpomene,
> May these verses be savored by you,
> Love commands it, Love has written it . . .

What they have never quoted—or even discussed—is the rest of the poem, with its peculiar implication. The poet goes on to decry the sorrowful state of the theatre where Amour has come to visit only to find it taken over by the heretic cult of his enemies, with their leader "accompanied by his garlanded darling boys." This rival, once adored in Sodom and Gomorrah, had gone on to Greece where he "instructed Socrates and Plato more than once," then to Rome and Florence, always seeking out the most cultured peoples: "and now he appears in Lutetia [the

90

Roman name for Paris], infamous abode of licentious desires which, where pleasure is concerned, is the equal of Italy and Greece."

This enemy god appears in the guise of a human who, in gentle bearing, delicate air, and clever speech, strongly resembles a certain marquis: "Thirty laughing *mignons* are in his service/Phyllis, observing this, flees with a sigh." Amour has fled the theatre in despair and Chloe is the only one with the power to make him return:

> He hovers above us
> When, as Phèdre or Monime,
> You share, with Racine,
> The legitimate tribute
>   of our incense.

The poet finally advises Chloe:

> Convert those who have bowed their knees
> Before the idol of Amour's rival;
> Amour made you priestess of the Temple;
> You must preach an example to the heretic.
> Preach without delay and quickly
> Come to sacrifice to the real Amour.

Having resigned himself to seeing Adrienne's favors bestowed upon others, Voltaire appears to be pleading to her to put those favors to good use. If he cannot have her, why at least does she not give herself over to the conversion of those *mignons fleuris?* The *Anti-Giton* originally had been entitled *La Courcillonnade,* and then *Verses against Monsieur de Courcillon.* Amour's enemy was actually Philippe Egon, son of Louis de Courcillon, Marquis de Dangeau.

Voltaire's works and correspondence abound with reference to Adrienne's acting style. In 1723, he immortalized her in his well-known *Epître a Mlle Lecouvreur:*

> The happy talent with which you charm France
> Had gleamed within you since your childhood
>   days.
> From that time on it was dangerous to see you,
> And you gave pleasure without even knowing it.
> Upon the stage you were fortunately led;
> Amidst the good wishes of a hundred fervent
>   hearts
> You recited, instructed by nature:
> It was a great deal, but not at all enough.
> You still needed a greater master;
> Permit me please to make known here
> The name of this God whose enchanting art
> Has given you your supreme glory.
> Tender Cupid has told me himself.
> I will be told that Cupid is a liar,
> Alas! I know he must not be trusted.
> Who, more than I, knows his perfidy?
> Who suffers more from his disloyalty?
> I shall never in my life believe that Child.
> But this time he has spoken the truth:
> This same Cupid, Venus, and Melpomene
> Were traveling far from Paris one day.
> These charming deities arrived at a place
> Where your allure was blossoming upon the stage.
> Each of the three with astonishment
> Witnessed that both simple and natural grace
> Which being then your only ornaments,
> Well deserved, without delay
> Our bestowal of all our treasures.
> A God's wish is done in an instant:
> At once the tragic Goddess
> Inspired in you taste, feeling,

Pathos and delicacy.
"I," said Venus, "will make her a gift
More precious, and that is the gift of pleasing.
She will enhance the Realm of Cythera,
The sight of her will trouble all hearts,
All great wits will come to pay her homage."
—"I," said Cupid, "I will do more:
I want her to love." Hardly had he spoken,
When in an instant you became perfect:
Without any care, without study or artifice,
You became the interpreter of the Passions.
O adorable subject of Cupid,
Forget not the secret of your art.[3]

In spite of the several names which have been amorously associated with Adrienne's, she refused most offers of this nature. To some she counter-offered with friendship, as one of her suitors, the Abbé Aunillon Delaunay du Gué, confirmed in his *Mémoires*. To his proposal Adrienne replied that she was: "intent only on making friends" and that she "feared attracting lovers. . . ."

"I took leave of her well resolved to follow her advice," the Abbé continued, "for in effect, I found her worthy of the friendship of the most well-bred people. My other sentiments, in all their passion, either cooled down or turned to friendship which was reciprocal between us until her death."

In warm yet eloquent language, Adrienne advised another suitor: "If I cannot make you happier, I feel the hurt more than you. I reproach myself much more strongly than you would find it in your heart to reproach me; but I could not deceive you. Capriciousness has nothing to do with reason, and love is a madness which, most assuredly, I shall do my best to avoid. You will find love

93

again and then the injustices you have suffered at my hand will only serve to make you happier. Permit me to suggest and advise—do be my friend, for of that I am worthy, but choose an entirely new heart for a mistress. May she still be in that blissful state of confidence which makes everything so beautiful; may she not yet have been betrayed or cast aside; may she see you as you are and want to compare all others with you; may she be young and strong enough to be mistress of her moods; and finally, may she procure for you the faithfulness I would have had, had I loved no one but you, and if you had loved me as much as you can, thereby winning me."

We do not know to whom this letter was addressed, but among the adorers she had to discourage—and of whom she succeeded in making friends—there are two whose names are well-known in the history of eighteenth-century France: La Chalotais and d'Argental.

Louis-René de Caraduc de la Chalotais, born in 1701, was in 1719 the future Procureur-Général of the Parlement of Brittany. In steady attendance at the Comédie-Française, he had courted Adrienne rather insistently, with no satisfaction.

For d'Argental, the transition from love to friendship was not quite so simple. It took a long series of crises before a solid friendship could finally be established, but again, it was a relationship that would last until the end of their lives.

Charles-Augustin de Ferriol d'Argental was born in 1700 and was seventeen when he first met Adrienne during her earliest days with the Comédie-Française. She considered him honest, dependable, and loyal. For him sacrifice was a vocation. He not only loved the theatre and literature, but he served them both well through his talent as, what we may call, a business agent. A lifelong friend of Voltaire as well, he managed the financial affairs of both actress and author with a scrupulous hand. A nineteenth-century historian once wrote that d'Argental was known for "his imperturbable friendship for the author of *Candide* and for his having subjected himself to the glory of the great poet. For long years this excellent man was observed to be impassioned for the affairs of the theatre, but, born invincibly for lesser roles, he devoted himself with an equal lack of self-interest to caring for the daughters of Adrienne and the tragedies of Voltaire."

At the time of their first meeting, Adrienne was still determined to avoid new love entanglements, but this had no effect on the youth who at once fell violently in love with her. Adrienne obstinately refused, not hesitating, however, to tender her counter-offer. Using every resource at her command to have him accept her on her own terms, she was attentive and persevering, offering him everything except what he really wanted. It took several years for d'Argental to understand the value of her consolation prize, but when he did, he proved himself to be the friend par excellence. Through a decisive act, Adrienne proved herself to be a worthy friend. D'Argental learned of this gesture long years after her death.

In June 1717, at the beginning of their relationship, Adrienne ended one of her letters cheerfully: "I absolutely want to have supper at your place Sunday or Monday. Farewell. Forgive me for my mood. Lord knows I forgive much where you are concerned—I was going to say that I forgive you for your love and remembered that you look upon me only as a friend, and that this is the only way I want you to look upon me." In almost all her letters to d'Argental there are some gracious references to the "conventions" not yet agreed to by him. Several months later the young man was in London where his family, disturbed over his behavior with an actress, had sent him. With his mother's consent Adrienne wrote him long, affectionate letters which were both witty and lighthearted, and which carefully avoided any reference to his feelings for her. Instead, she provided him with news of the goings-on in Paris, especially of the startling economic developments. For this was the time of John Law and his *système*.

At the death of Louis XIV, the public debt had risen to two billion, four hundred million *livres*. There remained in the royal treasury less than eight hundred thousand, and for the current year the deficit rose seventy-eight million, the following year's receipts having already been spent. There was little cash, faltering commerce, a nobility encumbered with debts, pensioners deprived of their revenue, and vast regions of the countryside deserted. The Regent, rejecting Saint-Simon's proposal for bankruptcy, sent for John Law, his old companion in debauchery and reputed to be a financial wizard, to rescue the State.

In May 1716, Law created a bank which succeeded in ending usury, restoring confidence in the business world, and maintaining the exchange rate in France's favor. For all this he was given the exclusive privilege to develop the French territories of Louisiana and, in 1717, founded the Compagnie d'Occident which immediately floated shares for the exploitation of the Mississippi valley, where it was thought silver and gold abounded. In May of 1719

Law combined the three companies of the Indies, China, and the Occident to create the Nouvelle Compagnie des Indes, and the shares, originally issued at 500 *livres*, had in October of 1719 reached 18,000!

There was a mad rush to the rue Quincampoix, then the banking center of Paris, where a furious business in speculation grew by leaps and bounds and where fortunes were made in several hours.

Aware of the danger to his system threatened by speculation, Law combined the Nouvelle Compagnie des Indes, in February of 1720, with his bank, in an effort to forestall it. Unfortunately, this caused the failure of both institutions and brought on the downfall of the *système*.

The speculative dealings on the rue Quincampoix had reached such a frenzy that the strict measures taken to prevent it were useless. Great luxury and wild spending were the rage of the hour. Robbery and murder were rampant, and Adrienne, who also engaged in the fashionable speculation, lost no time in reporting to d'Argental, who appears to have sat out the whole affair in London, the execution of the Count de Horn:

March 27, 1720

> The shares were changed to the Compagnie d'Occident, and those of the Occident were converted to the Compagnie des Indes. The entire issue is now fixed at 9,000 *livres* per share. I still have two of this type that I am advised to hold on to. Yesterday, Monsieur le Count de Horn was executed for having robbed and assassinated someone in the rue Quincampoix. The matter seems to have been resolved as promptly as simple prudence required. His family and

97

relatives solicited the Regent in his favor, but in
vain. The Regent himself is his mother's cousin,
which made the Count the Regent's grandnephew.
All the Lorraines, Montmorencys, Bouillons,
Bournonvilles, d'Isanguiens, to say nothing of the
German princes, were related to the poor man
and were proud of it. He had an income of
12,000 *livres* and a brother whose income was
1,000 *écus* and who begged him to come live with
him. The Count had been in Paris for two months
and this is not the only crime for which he was
accused. He was only 22 years old. They broke
him on the wheel in the Place de Grèves
yesterday, together with one of his friends who
was a Captain and Chevalier of Saint-Louis
named V[ictor] de M[illy]. Because of this
incident the rue Quincampoix has been closed.
It is strictly forbidden to assemble there and there
are guards on foot and on horseback who have
been enforcing the regulations since the murder.
An endless amount of other murders, thefts, and
crimes, whether true or false, is the subject of
all conversation in Paris these days. All coinage is
going to be prohibited with the exception of the
petit louis d'argent which will be struck and will
have a value of three *livres*. . . .

Obviously the threat of the terrible breaking on the wheel
in the presence of morbid sightseers did nothing to allay
the rampant crime.

When the *débâcle* finally occurred in December of
1720, it swept all before it. John Law was nearly torn to
pieces in the streets by the Parisian populace. The Regent
allowed him to flee the country and to take with him
only the few hundred *livres* remaining to him. He landed

in Brussels later that month and nine years later died a poor man in Venice.

Notwithstanding the impersonal nature of her letters to d'Argental in London, his trip there did not have the desired effect, and his family, more alarmed than before, decided to send him to the island of Santo Domingo in the West Indies. Adrienne, horrified at this prospect, implored Madame de Ferriol, his mother, not to proceed with her plans.

To quote from the nineteenth-century critic Sainte-Beuve, Madame de Ferriol was the "worthy sister of Mme de Tencin, and this is all that it is necessary to say about Mme de Ferriol." Madame de Tencin, incidentally, had been mistress to the Regent and then to Cardinal Dubois —to whom she bore an illegitimate son whom she at once abandoned. The child, brought up by the wife of a poor glazier, was to become famous under the name of d'Alembert.

Adrienne's letter to Mme de Ferriol is the pearl of her correspondence, embodying the noble tone so appropriate to her intent:

Paris, March 22, 1721

Madame,

It is not without great pain that I learn of your anxiety and of the plans you are making as a result. I have been equally grieved I might add to hear that you blame my conduct; but I am writing to you less to justify it than to protest to you that, in the future, in all that is of interest to you, it shall be such as you may wish to prescribe. Tuesday I had asked permission to see you in

order to speak to you in confidence and to ask
for your commands. But your manner of receiving
me destroyed my zeal and I found myself only
timid and sad in your presence. It is necessary,
however, that you should know my true sentiments, and, if you will allow me to add, that you
should not disdain to hear my very humble
remonstrances, if you do not wish to lose your
son.

He is the most respectful, the most honorable
young man I have ever met in my life. How you
would admire him if he were not a part of you!
Once again, Madame, deign to join with me in
destroying the weakness which irritates you, but
in which I have no part, whatever you may say.
Do not be bitter or scornful toward him. In spite
of the tender friendship, and the veneration I hold
for him, I would rather take upon myself all his
hatred, than expose him to the least temptation
which might cause him to lose his respect for you.
You are too much interested in curing him not to
be anxious to attain your objective. But your
very eagerness makes you unable to attain it alone,
especially when you seek to put an end to his
love by an attitude of authority, or by painting
me in a disadvantageous light, whether true or
not. This passion must surely be extraordinary,
since it has existed so long a time without hope, in
the midst of disappointments, in spite of the
voyages you have made him undertake, and of
eight months' stay in Paris without seeing me—at
least not at my house—and when he had no reason
to believe I should ever receive him again. I
thought he was cured, and therefore consented to
see him during my last illness. It is easy to believe
that seeing him would give me infinite pleasure
were it not for this unhappy passion, which
astonishes as much as it flatters me, and of which

I refuse to take advantage. You fear that by seeing me he will forget his duties, and you push this fear to the point of making violent decisions against him. In truth, Madame, it is not just that he be rendered unhappy in so many ways. Do not add to my own severity toward him; seek rather to lighten his burden. Make all his resentment fall upon me, but let him find consolation in your kindness.

I will write to him whatever you please; I will never see him again if you desire it; I will even go away into the country if you deem it necessary. But do not threaten to send him to the end of the world. He could be useful to his country; he will be the delight of his friends; he will fill you with satisfaction and cover you with glory; you only have to guide his talents and let his virtues act for themselves. Forget for a while that you are his mother, if maternity is in any way opposed to the kindness which, on my knees, I beg you to show him. Finally, Madame, I would rather retire from the world, or love him out of passion, than allow that he be further tormented for or by me. Grant your forgiveness to a feeling which you can destroy, but upon which I can have no effect. Add what I now beg of you to all the other acts of kindness you have bestowed upon me, and allow me to think that my sincere attachment and my lively gratitude will make you keep for me the kindly feeling which I so value; and permit me to congratulate myself throughout life on being, with profound respect, Madame, your very humble and very obedient servant,

Adrienne Lecouvreur.

P.S. Let me know what you wish me to do. If you desire to speak to me without his knowing it, I

> will meet you wherever you please, Madame, and
> will spare no pains, no efforts, in order that you
> may be satisfied with both your son and me.

D'Argental would see this letter for the first time when
he was eighty-four years of age. He came upon it by ac-
cident in his mother's old desk, and it may well be believed that on reading it he burst into tears.

Whether moved by Adrienne's plea or by reasons of
self-interest, the Ferriol family did not go through with
its plans. D'Argental thereafter conducted himself nobly
and gave his family no further cause to worry. Once
Adrienne was certain that d'Argental was finally over his
passion, she would often remind him how much she prized
their new relationship: "Never tire of being wise nor of
loving me. What I feel for you is worth more than the
most violent and disordered passion." She could promise
her everlasting friendship despite a feeling of approaching
death brought on by an unyielding weakness:

> May the length of my life be the term of your
> devotion, my dear friend. There is perhaps hardly
> enough time left for you to be devoted, and I
> will always regret my severity and shall never
> cease in my admiration of your virtues. Perhaps,
> too, if my life lasts longer than I believe it will,
> you will one day find, in my tender and un-
> alterable friendship, support against passions, to
> which time and your age will lead you. You may
> even become religious. Finally, in whatever way
> we can manage it, let us be friends until death.

No doubt the word "severity" referred to the friendship
ideal which Adrienne imposed upon those she considered

her friends. Well aware that her demands were difficult for some, she herself often suffered from her severity:

> You send a messenger to me without writing to me yourself? and you set off on a trip without seeing me? Admit it, my dear friend, I am in the act of being forgotten, and soon I will no longer be able to count on you. I . . . cannot resign myself to the thought of not seeing you at all. I miss you now more than ever. You are taking good revenge on my injustices, and I am beginning to think that yours surpass mine by a good deal. . . . Writing this has calmed me and I was never more imbued with the feeling of friendship, tenderness, and respect. Farewell, don't forget me completely, or at least don't let me think so. . . . Take care of yourself scrupulously. I demand it in the name of that which interests you most in the world.

Even after d'Argental had become Councillor in Parlement, the Ferriol family was still concerned with the important place Adrienne occupied in his life. Rumor had it that d'Argental had rights in Adrienne's house other than those of a friend, and since there appeared to be nothing improbable about this type of arrangement, it was generally believed. But, as with Voltaire, we know that d'Argental never had such rights. These were reserved for Maurice de Saxe, whom Adrienne had met late in the year 1720.

If d'Argental and Voltaire ever complained of Adrienne's strengthening relationship with Maurice, there certainly is no evidence of this. In fact, both "suitors" struck up their own personal friendships with the Saxon noble who was later to become Maréchal de France. However, a certain Mademoiselle whose name is unknown was not at all happy with Adrienne's developing romance, and this had nothing to do with the young lady's own interest in Maurice. She did not even know him. Her interest was in the direction of Adrienne, and the least conclusion we may draw from a series of letters written to her by Adrienne would be one that permitted us to say that the two ladies were on the closest of terms:

[*end of 1720*]

I wanted to ask you to supper today; but as you are going to the country, I intend having supper elsewhere and want you to enjoy yourself where you are going. It is certain that you will greatly please those who have the honor of supping with you. In my opinion, it is dangerous to see you; I cannot any longer bear the other women, and it would be much worse if I should see you less often surrounded by people who steal half of your attentions—that is to say, half of my pleasure. However, it is not fair that I be an obstacle to yours or to those who, as I, do you just homage. Have no more doubts about my constancy. It will not be I who would fail you first; and were you in the Palace of Glory, to my detriment and despite my envy, I would still love you. Don't work up any silly idea about that fantasy you imagine will bring you new misfortunes, and which portends a kind of happiness for me. A silly little nothing could make me more unhappy than I have yet been, and you can only hope for better; besides, you can defy envy and even destiny. But all my prudence and all the attention I give to my good conduct cannot prevent accidents against which my sensibility will not grow tough. You have only to draw on your own resources, perhaps you will reach the moment I desire and that you merit. Whatever flattery you may reserve for me, I shall always appear unconcerned, even if it had all the effect you hoped for. There are very sweet errors to which I can no longer give myself. Too sad experiences have enlightened my reason. Adieu, I embrace you, I love you, and shall love you all my life. I'll see you as soon as possible. In the meantime, think of me.

Elements in this first letter offer interesting biographical possibilities. Indications in the ensuing letters would permit us to date them between 1721 and 1723, or at the beginning of Adrienne's relationship with Maurice de Saxe. This would explain the overall tone of the above letter: an effort to assure its recipient that although Adrienne's attentions lie in another's direction, there is no reason to doubt her continued love for the recipient: "Have no more doubts about my constancy. . . . I will always love you. Don't work up any silly idea about that fantasy you imagine will bring you new misfortunes, and which portends a kind of happiness for me." If Adrienne does not respond to the lady's flattery, she assures her that this does not mean that the lady's compliments did not have their desired effect. Adrienne wishes only to avoid further sentimental errors: "Whatever flattery you may reserve for me, I shall always appear unconcerned. . . . There are very sweet errors to which I can no longer give myself."

But the lady in question must have had further reason to doubt Adrienne's faithfulness, and we must assume that she made Adrienne aware of her doubts. Further letters in the series contain such remonstrances as: "You are wrong to complain of me, my dear friend. I love you more than any woman I know, and I flatter myself, too, that you love me more than any other woman." "If you have as much constancy and friendship for me as I find grace and wit in you, I am too happy. . . . Everything becomes you, even madness, and I know of nothing that can resist you and which does not even applaud its own defeat. Why were you not my first love? I would still be faithful."

In the end, Adrienne's love for Maurice was destined to leave no time for Mademoiselle, who appears to have made her feelings on this score understood. Adrienne replied: "Be quiet, you impertinent thing! I am neither ungrateful nor unfaithful . . . at present I am concerned with completely different matters; but, whatever you say, I am thinking of you, and I love you because I want to . . . do I have to say it again? Count on me or—enough. Adieu."

The lady in question was clearly someone of high social standing who must have shown her love for Adrienne in many material ways. Why else would Adrienne have to protest accusations of ingratitude and opportunism: "I am neither ungrateful nor unfaithful. . . . I love you because I want to."

The suggestion of homosexuality as it applies here should not be glossed over. That actresses of the Comédie-Française engaged in Sapphic practices did not thus set them apart from the rest of society. It would appear that they were merely following a fashion of the time which opened new doors—for them at least. In eighteenth-century France sexual inversion would appear to have been as commonplace as it is in all modern society.

There is an abundance of historic documents which serves to quash any doubt in this respect. Elisabeth-Charlotte, the Regent's mother, was given to seeing Lesbianism rampant in every direction and in her proverbial bluntness accused many of her contemporaries—from Christine of Sweden to Madame de Maintenon herself—of preferring their own sex.

Even the ill-destined Marie-Antoinette, later in the century, would not be spared this manner of gossip. Both in rumor and in scandalous, often pornographic pamphlets printed anonymously, the following ladies were said to be among her lovers: the Duchesse de Pecquigny, Mme de Saint-Mégrin, the Princesse de Guémené, the Duchesse de Polignac, the Comtesse de la Motte, the Princesse de Lamballe, Mme Toursel, and the following actresses: Mlle Dorvat, Mlle Miséry, Mlle Bertin, Mlle Guimard, Sophie Arnould, and Mlle Raucourt. Historians rarely fail to mention this gossip about Marie-Antoinette, but they are quick to qualify such assertions as calumny.

If the easy morals of actresses led them to accept love from either sex, we cannot say that Adrienne Lecouvreur differed in this respect from her colleagues. Her relationship with Mademoiselle was not totally one of anguish, and there is at least one letter, written sometime in 1722, which shows the lighter side of their friendship. We note the care taken by Adrienne not to wound Mlle's feelings:

> I am not at all annoyed with you for letting two weeks go by without giving me a single sign of the friendship with which you flatter me. If your silence is forgivable, mine must speak in my favor. I cannot imagine, however, what may be causing you to be chagrined with me. Without delving

for the cause, it suffices for me to know that I
have nothing for which to reproach myself, and I
believe, after all, that it is not so bad as you
make it out to be.

I am absolutely counting on you for tomorrow.
Even though we will be only two couples, this
must not alarm your delicacy; just ready yourself
for a triumph, for you shall have a great wit
and a philosopher to combat, as well as a friend
to help out. Besides,

> *Pour ne vous point flatter,*
> *Je vous donne à combattre un homme*
> *à redouter.*

[from *Le Cid*, I, 5: "So as not to flatter you,
I give you a fearsome man to fight."]

He is Monsieur de Fontenelle for whom I must
admit I have taken quite a lively affection. I
should like to please him and it is through you
that I intend to succeed. The philosopher (Du
Marsais) will perhaps seem very dull, but they
say that he knows how to argue a point, and if he
by chance should bore you, one of your glances
will suffice to confuse him, for I have heard it
said that his philosophy does not prevent him
from being sensitive, nor his sensitivity from being
respectful. Thus you have nothing to fear. . . .
Do not try to talk me out of this get-together.

We know that by this time Du Marsais had success-
fully coached Adrienne in matters of diction. But Mademoiselle must certainly have fulfilled Adrienne's ex-
pectations. Bernard le Bovier de Fontenelle, that lion of
the great salons of the day, became a regular member of
Adrienne's circle. He was the nephew of the great Corneille. Born in 1657, he would live for two months short

of one hundred years and was thus a living and direct link between the *Grand Siècle* of Louis XIV and the eighteenth century. He wrote poems, operas, and tragedies, but found his true forte in the popularization of science. In this vein his *Entretiens sur la pluralité des mondes* is his most famous work.

In the salons a popular way to pass the time was in the creation of "portraits" or word pictures of well-known personalities—often people who were themselves present when the portrait was recited. Here is a portrait of Fontenelle which has been attributed to Adrienne herself:

> Unknown persons do little honor to those about whom they speak and I shall not dare to reveal what I think of M. de Fontenelle; but I cannot refuse myself in secret the pleasure of painting him here as he appears to me.

> His physiognomy first announces his wit; a worldly air, covering his entire person, renders him kind in everything he does.

> When a mind is embellished, what is essential is often excluded; unique in his species, he combines everything necessary for the love and respect of integrity. Straightforwardness, fairness make up his character. A vivid and brilliant imagination, fine and delicate turns of phrase, new and always well-chosen expressions are its adornments. A pure heart, flawless behavior, uniform conduct, and principles concerning all, demanding little, justifying everything, always seizing upon the good, so quickly abandoning what is bad that one doubts that he ever noticed it; difficult to acquire but more difficult to lose; exact in friendship,

scrupulous in love. The *honnête-homme* is nowhere neglected, he is proper in the most delicate
of exchanges, although he is the delight of the
learned. Modest in his discourse, simple in his
actions, the superiority of his merit is evident, but
he never makes it felt.

Such gifts easily persuade one of the calmness
of his soul; he keeps it in so strong a peace that
the disease of envy has not yet been powerful
enough to shake it.

Finally, one could say of him what has already
been said of an illustrious person: he does honor
to mankind, and if his virtues do not make him
immortal, they at least make him very worthy of
being so.[4]

Chapter Six

MAURICE DE SAXE
1720–1725

ERMANN-MAURICE, Comte de Saxe, was the legitimized bastard son of Augustus, then Elector of Saxony, and Countess Maria-Aurora von Königsmark, a Swedish beauty of noble birth. She had gone to Dresden in 1694 to seek the intervention of Augustus in favor of her brother, Count Philipp Christoph von Königsmark who had disappeared after being accused of an intrigue with Sophia Dorothea, the wife of Elector George Louis of Hanover (later George I of England). It is believed that Count Philipp Christoph was killed by order of the Elector of Hanover. In Dresden Aurora became the mistress of Augustus, whose physical prowess was equalled only by his lack of principle: he abandoned Aurora after a short-lived liaison—which ended with the birth of Maurice on October 28, 1696, in Goslar.

In 1699, Peter I of Russia, Frederick IV of Denmark, and Maurice's father (who by this time had become Augustus II, King of Poland) entered into an alliance against Charles XII of Sweden. In 1700, when Maurice was four, the desire of Sweden's neighbors to break her supremacy in the Baltic area—and particularly Peter the Great's conflicting ambitions with Charles XII—led to

111

the outbreak of the Northern War. "The dear, little mysterious one," as his mother called him, grew up in the midst of international hostilities, being shuttled back and forth from Hamburg to Berlin to Leipzig.

In spite of this, Aurora—who had the singular talent of speaking the languages of several countries she had never visited and who wrote French verse which, according to Voltaire, could have been written "by a person born at Versailles"—looked after the education of her son with loving tenderness. In his *Mémoires*, Maurice spoke of this military infancy and told of the frustration of his tutors who resigned themselves to the impossibility of teaching him anything:

> When I was twelve I was made a soldier by my father who had found me to be of very strong constitution. He confided me to the legion he had presented the Emperor a year before. I took my oath on January 15, 1708, on the Plain of Lutzen in Saxony, known as the place where the late Gustavus-Adolphus died.

The childhood of a great soldier is always surrounded by legend, and there is no dearth of mythologizing where it concerns Maurice de Saxe. At the age of thirteen he is said to have participated in the Battle of Malplaquet against the armies of France, which he would command some thirty years hence as Maréchal de France. When he was sixteen, he married the Countess de Loben in Dresden, leaving her shortly thereafter under circumstances still not fully known. Preceded by a glorious reputation which placed him in no fewer than eleven campaigns in Poland, the Low Countries, and Pomerania, he arrived in Paris, in April of 1720, at the age of 24.

As a colonel, he was heartily welcomed by the Regent Duc d'Orléans who at once named him *maréchal de camp.* Shortly thereafter, having obtained from Dresden permission to join the service of France together with freedom from his marriage vows, Maurice purchased the Gréder Regiment which then took his name and became the Régiment de Saxe.

His average height gave no hint of his extraordinary strength. It was said that he could break a horseshoe in two with his bare hands. His bearing was noble, gentle, and martial. In the manner of a hero of antiquity, he fascinated all women. He already considered himself to be the pretender to the throne of Poland and was impudent to the point of endangering his hopes. He thus managed to fire the wrath of Count von Flemming, his father's favorite and prime minister, whom Voltaire called "an absolute minister." Much later in his life, having completely forgotten his momentary marriage with Countess de Loben, Madame de Pompadour would ask him why he never married, to which he would reply: "A woman is not proper baggage for a soldier." One of his biographers wrote: "He was a soldier in search of a kingdom." This search would take him from the desolate plains of Courland to the mountain crags of Corsica, and from the tropical lowlands of Madagascar to the virgin lands of America.

When he appeared in Paris, Adrienne had "closed her heart" to the suffering and joys she knew all too well: "There are sweet errors to which I can no longer give myself; experiences too sad have enlightened my reason." However, she had not reckoned with the prestige of the young, adventurous prince who had ignited the passions of an endless sequence of conquered ladies.

For Maurice, life under the Regency seemed celestial. All the important salons were opened to the young hero whose exploits were the subject of much elegant conversation. After seeing Adrienne for the first time in the role of Phèdre on the stage of the theatre on the rue des Fossés-Saint-Germain, he became an avid theatre-goer. Given to occasional sentimentality, he could love her for her gentle and honest nature. In him she saw a generous, affable, and compassionate being:

> I find you of admirable gentility and politeness, good, obliging, but not quite penetrated with what is truly called love, although you are occupied with its effects.

On September 13, 1720, Adrienne was not yet totally afflicted by the all-consuming commitment to him that would become legendary. Maurice returned to Dresden, but he found a Saxon Court greatly troubled by his adventures and not at all happy over the prospect of the new chapter it sensed he was about to add to the novel of his life. On top of this—and immediately after his arrival in Dresden—he involved himself in an adulterous affair which almost caused a complete break between him and his father Augustus. Adrienne, of course, was completely unaware of all this and could not have known Maurice's confused state of mind when she wrote:

> I have received, my handsome Count, the letter and the reproaches that you were kind enough to send me. In my note you read that you are as unjust as I am sensitive to the friendship you do me the honor of according me. You shall see . . . that I am not the only one to keep the

memory of your worth, and that here we have
as much constancy as taste. Give us proof of
yours, and that will crown the high idea we have
of your heart. All your other qualities are so
evident that all we need is the happy experience
for which you have given us reason to hope, to
believe that you are perfect and to make us feel
how happy one is to please you.

Your story of the pleasure of the Hague was
delicious. You should describe more often the
places you honor with your visits.

Farewell, my great Prince; receive with kindness the perfect assurances of my attachment and
gratitude, and let me have news of you often.

But shortly thereafter we can begin to see the complete
surrender that was to take place:

Yesterday I saw in you a fear which I am quite
resolved to reassure, even though it had ap-
preciably flattered me. Each of us is sensitive in
a very different way: you do not count on me
enough, and I am very afraid of counting on you
too much. However, I feel strongly that it is too
late to turn back and that I am more to you than
any other woman. You have had the intelligence
to know this and not to abuse it. You have chosen
the surest route to finally turn my head and to
give our understanding the most proper tone to
procure for us the most pleasure and happiness.
You are too accustomed to prompt and complete
victory not to be grateful to me for having prepared for you a different triumph that excites you
because of its uniqueness. It is for you that I
work, and one day you will discover what you
are losing today. I am nonetheless committed and
I hereby swear to you a fidelity in all things.

You are about to take a long trip and could
doubt me if you did not have this proof of my
courage; I would have reason to doubt you if I
had left you nothing to desire. If you return with
the same eagerness, what pleasure to satisfy it and
to have in your eyes the look of freshness! If
time or another fantasy destroys this taste you
exhibit for me, you will be all the less embarrassed
to leave me and I will less regret the loss of you.
But I will try to keep you, taking care to make
you remember your promises and to reiterate
mine to you. Finally, I will endeavor to prove to
you that I love you and in a most uncommon way.

Yesterday you asked if I would be at home at
four o'clock: would you be able to come at
three? I would thus see you an hour earlier and
doubtlessly with much more liberty. I may not
wish to succumb, but this does not mean that I
wish to see you any the less. . . . Why can't
you stay?

Farewell, send me a word in reply and try to
come at three.

In spite of the fact that Adrienne was forced to resign
herself to Maurice's numerous absences of varying dura-
tion, their relationship continued in a state of near-bliss
for three or four years.

Sunday, October 1, 1724.

I shall die of boredom if you do not return, my
dear Count: the length of your absence baffles
me. I await you at every moment and have been
doing so since Wednesday, and the more you
postpone your return, the more I hope to see you
entering my room. I received a letter from you
on Tuesday, but you do not tell me either what

you are doing or when you will return. Don't
you blame yourself for that precious time you are
wasting far from me? How can I believe in your
love after all that?

But in the previous May, Adrienne had written in a much
more despondent tone:

I am very much upset at not seeing you. All I
have are gloomy and sorrowful ideas since your
absence, and I have never wanted anything more
than your return. I am outraged that you do not
write to me at all. Can one love and be so neglectful? Is one word so difficult to write? Just one
word from your hand would calm my worries;
but my anger cannot prevail over the consolation
I find in complaining about you. Take advantage
of it, if you wish, I cannot prevent it.

She continues this letter with some newsworthy items:

Smallpox is beginning to renew its effects: the
Prince de Soubise (Jules-François-Louis de Rohan,
Prince de Soubise, grandson of the Duchesse de
Ventadour) died of it yesterday. Many more
have died and perhaps so shall I before your
return.

Even here, Adrienne could not refrain from using the
news to her own advantage:

If I have smallpox and if I should die of it, you
will lose more than a mistress because I feel that
I value you through a most loving and solid
friendship which it will depend on you to conserve so long as I live. I mentioned my gloomy

117

ideas, but that is what you have caused by your absence and silence. I was so happy before your departure; won't you soon bring back those wonderful days? I don't know why I am more troubled during this trip than during the one you made to your own country. [In May of 1724 Maurice went to Holland and England, where mysterious plans needed his attention.] Apparently I love you even more, or else present evils always seem more considerable than those of the past. Besides, I don't like your staying longer than you said you would. I hate all deception, however innocent it be, and cannot suffer your not always telling me the truth.

Farewell; I do not wish to prolong this troubled letter. If I should have a moment of good humor, I'll write to you in another tone. Farewell! I wish you the best of health and many honest pleasures; but do return.

By this time Adrienne had become involved in Maurice's great designs, whatever they may have been. At the death of the Regent in 1723, the Duc de Bourbon had become Prime Minister and together with his mistress, Madame de Prie, was treating affairs of state in a most capricious and therefore unpopular manner. It was they who convinced young King Louis XV to send his fiancée, the Infanta, back to Spain and to marry instead a princess of their own choosing, the Polish Marie Leszenska. (Moreover, the Infanta had not yet reached puberty, and so the court wanted a fertile fiancée *quickly*, lest Louis XV pass away, leaving no heir to the throne.) Adrienne induced Maurice to pay homage to the powerful Duc de Bourbon and was uncompromising in her

zeal to make a true sovereign of the illegitimate son of a
King:

> Good evening, my very dear Count. I have
> just sent away two very generous strangers who
> had done me the honor to have supper with me—
> this, in order to write to you. If I had foreseen
> your letter, I never would have kept them so long.
> However, it would have been difficult to avoid,
> since they came in person, begging to be admitted.
> I call "strangers" those who have not been ini-
> tiated into our mysteries. I read your letter
> while they were here because it had been given
> to me at table during supper, and I could not
> put off reading it. But I wanted to be alone to
> answer in comfort. I adored you all of today,
> and I believe I flatter myself to think that if you
> had been able to guess how much I desired you,
> you would have come in spite of your trip.
>
> It seems that I have a hundred thousand things
> to tell you. Your long trip which I at first gently
> accepted has since saddened me despite my desire
> that you profit from it. I have so keenly felt the
> horror of a long absence that the present one
> seems unbearable. Besides, I desired you; a *je ne
> sais quoi* was probing at my heart; and I would
> have done unbelievable things to see you today.
> If I were not afraid to write in a scandalous way,
> I would add that I would have embraced you
> with my entire soul and, if I saw you at this
> instant, I would continue to do so. . . . I said
> to myself: "He's busy with his horses and gives
> no thought to me." What an occupation, and
> what do triumphs in which I have no part matter
> to me?
>
> I will go Tuesday to the agreed spot, and would

go further if you so wished. I will see you there,
but will be upset at having to return alone. Won't
you ever leave the Court [at Versailles]? Won't
you come here [to Paris]? Do you remember
everything you told me? Have your triumphs
erased that melancholy you affected and those so
flattering feelings you expressed to me? Reassure
me, console me, relieve me of all I suffer and of
what your unbearable trips have yet to make me
endure. Farewell, dear Count. If I followed my
own advice, and my letters pleased as much as
those of Mlle de la Motte, I would write you more
often. [Marie-Hélène des Mottes, called Mlle de
la Motte, actress of the Comédie-Française, born
in 1704, made her debut in 1722; obviously there
was some question here about a relationship between her and Maurice.] But on this point I
must not forget myself.

In spite of Adrienne's noble intent, she could not re-
press the gnawing, perhaps well-founded, suspicion and
jealousy brought on by the long intervals of silence on
Maurice's part. He sometimes would attempt to justify
his own infidelities by pointing an accusing finger at
Adrienne. She attempted to explain her reaction to this
type of accusation:

Return then, and have no further fears of ever
repenting your love for me. I will commit you
to nothing which might be contrary to your
fortune or happiness: I will even sacrifice mine as
well as my life. Stop tormenting yourself in vain.
Don't accuse me, for I am no longer myself when
I am suspected by you or by anyone. My first
reaction is to be grieved before defending myself,
and I think that truth must always speak in my

Adrienne Lecouvreur, engraving by Schmidt
after painting by Fontaine

*A presumed portrait of Mlle Champmeslé,
Adrienne's great predecessor*

THE COMEDIE FRANÇAISE : FRANÇOISE FOLIOT

Adrienne's chief rival:
Mlle Duclos (Marie-Anne de Châteauneuf).
"Whether in roles of Corneille
or Racine, love was so well copied
that as Theseus' lover or wife, she always
brought forth from the soul either terror or pity"

THE COMEDIE FRANÇAISE : FRANÇOISE FOLIOT

The theatre on the rue des Fossés-Saint-Germain in 1726

THE COMEDIE FRANÇAISE : FRANÇOISE FOLIOT

A production of Quinault and Lully's THÉSÉE

THE BETTMANN ARCHIVE

Adrienne Lecouvreur in the role of Cornélie,
from Corneille's LA MORT DE POMPÉE.
Drevet FILS engraving taken
from the Coypel painting after her death.

Charlotte Desmares
"Her tears were touching, her laugh was piquant; she was equally mistress in both genres. . . ."

*Michel Baron, who came
out of retirement to appear with Adrienne*

François-Marie Arouet de Voltaire

THE COMEDIE FRANÇAISE : FRANÇOISE FOLIOT

John Law, the Scotsman whose
financial manipulations created the
"Compagnie D'Occident" bubble.
When it finally burst in 1720, he had
to flee the country

*Augustus "The Strong," Elector
of Saxony and later King of Poland*

Maurice de Saxe, Augustus'
illegitimate son and later Maréchal de France,
the great love of Adrienne's life

Alexis Piron. "Here is Piron who was nothing, not even an Academician."

Mlle Duclos, painting by Largillière

THE COMEDIE FRANÇAISE : FRANÇOISE FOLIOT

Adrienne Lecouvreur's note to her colleagues at the
Comédie-Française: "Je suplie la Compagnie de
ne point conter sur moy pour jeudi dans BRITTANICUS
sy Mlle Aubert y joue Agrippine. Sy l'on peut
engager Mademoiselle Dangeville a avoir la bonté
de jouer Junie on me fera grand plaisir, mais rien ne
me poura déterminer à changer la résolution que
j'ay prise de ne point jouer avec Mlle Aubert."

(I beg the Company not to count on me Thursday in
BRITTANICUS if Mlle Aubert is playing Agrippine.
If Mlle Dangeville would be good enough to
play Junie I would be very pleased, but nothing can
change my determination not to play with
Mlle Aubert)

THE COMEDIE FRANÇAISE : FRANÇOISE FOLIOT

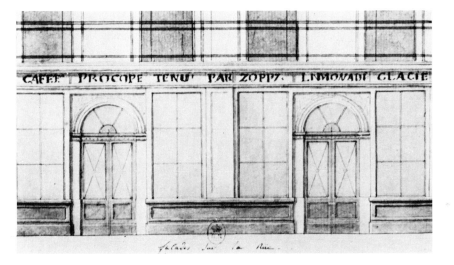

Facade of the Café Procope, as it appeared in the
18th century. Here the Abbé Bouret met
Duchemin, Duclos' young husband, in what was
perhaps the beginning of the conspiracy against
Adrienne's life

THE COMEDIE FRANÇAISE: FRANÇOISE FOLIOT

❖

An incarnation of the legend:
Rachel (Elisa Félix) in the title role
of ADRIENNE LECOUVREUR

favor. Just as I am disconcerted in bad company
and only appear to be myself in good company,
so can my feelings, my delicacy, my attachment,
show themselves only when they are believed
in, when I am respected. Haven't you tried? Am
I made to be treated like the majority of other
women, in any offhanded manner? The friends
you see me with, my conduct, past and present,
with respect to them and, more than that, the
natural admiration and my taste for true merit
as well as your great qualities, don't they divulge
a soul which is above the vulgar?

In the midst of all these comings and goings of an adventurous soldier, how can we discern those times in
which absence had become most intolerable?

It was during this period that we have the often-repeated evidence of Adrienne's early illnesses. Already in
February and March 1721, her painful fits of dizziness
obliged her to be absent from performances. Her earliest
biographer reported that four years before her death
"she underwent a dysentry of which, according to the
opinion of the most famous doctors, she could not be
cured, and which brought her close to the grave."

Paris, November 5, 1724.

Affliction has finally come about. My chest has
become inflamed, oppression and spitting of
blood followed. Then the remedies—bleedings,
milk, and all the apparatus of a sickness which
would be even more considerable if I had not
sought some gentle relief. I confided my pain to
Rochemore, and after having shown him this
letter and made known my sadness and resentment, he did so much by means of his good

121

discourse, that he persuaded me that you are less wrong than I had thought. He reminded me of everything that can reassure me, and our conversations always end with my thinking well of you again. This is the sole remedy I believe salutary to my deplorable health; but how much worry I still have! You do not write at all, you will take a thousand years to return, and who knows how you will think on your return, or how you think even now. Everything here speaks to me of you, and nothing where you are speaks to you of me.

I become ill to think that four months still remain before you return, and I would not be able to express to you the difference there is between me and myself since you have left. As much as I have seen you, nothing has afflicted me more than the horror of this separation. Your presence spreads a charm over my pain, but at present there is nothing to relieve it. If only something could occur, some great event that would bring you back; if only I could fly to where you are. Oh, how unhappy, how incapable is my sex! Correctness and reason are in bad accord with the passions! But why don't you write at least, since that is the only resort remaining to us? Overcome your laziness if you want me to live. Don't await my reply in order to send me news of what you are doing and what is happening in your heart. Write me long letters and let them be always sincere. I want to know what you are doing every moment of my life. Farewell. An extreme weakness and a slight dizziness oblige me to end abruptly.

But the long-awaited letters did come from time to time. Unfortunately, there is no record of Maurice's let-

ters to Adrienne, but we may be assured that their effect
was to cure her of her pain, if only for the moment:

January 14, 1725.

Never could I believe that a letter would give
so much pleasure as the one I have just received
from you, my very dear Count. I don't know how
to express it, but its contents of love and sentiment have so keenly passed into my soul that
what I feel resembles nothing at all what one may
imagine. I am crying out of joy and love. I have
known true love in all you write, and my happiness has no comparison.

Here we are, my dear Count, at the point so
desired: you love me as I want to be loved, and I
love you as you merit. My health, my life are
in your hands and I give them over gladly. Yes,
I no longer wish to live except for you. I think
only of you, and I do for the remainder of my
life only what can convince you of my love. But
this will be done without demanding anything
of you which might disturb either your fortune,
your reputation, or your duties. If it is possible,
I wish to make up, through my conduct and
manner of thinking, for that which is lacking in
my face and condition, and for all the faults
which may be mine through no fault of my own.
I shall invent, I shall seek all that can justify your
love; and Love promises to serve me in this task
since I please you even from afar. Since you desire
to live with me all my life, you shall see how I
shall give myself to you. You will find in me the
alacrity of the most loving mistress, the security,
the understanding of a friend, the attachment and
the fidelity of the most respectful domestic, and
the interest of the mother and of the most reason-

123

able and dutiful wife. My soul, most naturally given to good, will not weaken your virtues, and I will sacrifice my sweetest pleasures to what will make you happy and respectable. Finally, my objective will always be to make you think, even when you have lost me, which can come about only by my death, that I was worthy of you through my heart.

You have put me at ease by telling me of your plans. Profit well from them, my dear Count, without neglecting any of your pleasures. Show yourself as you are; you will acquire new friends and will gather enemies. This is a good way to avenge oneself; and the surest way to arrive at your objective. You must take advantage of the time, I cannot repeat this too often. Don't torment yourself over the future, but think of it with reason. Enjoy the present, but do not abuse it—that is to say, amuse yourself because it is my wish. You love hunting—you must hunt. The King loves the table—you must keep him company. You can love me and also take pleasure in all you do—you only have to tell yourself "She wants it, she is happy when I am, even though she is far from me." Only stop once in a while when the occasion or mood would push you on, and tell yourself "If I endanger myself to the point of harm, she would be devastated: I wish to conserve myself for her and be esteemed by her." Finally, think of me in everything you do, in a way most proper for our happiness and for the tender, sincere, and unique love I have for you.

Farewell my king, my lord, my friend, my lover, my hero, and all I love and will love my whole life. Again, farewell, be happy for the love of me, I entreat you. You couldn't better prove your love than by doing what I recommend; and

> I couldn't better prove to you mine than by
> protesting to you at this moment that I believe
> you are faithful. But farewell, for I soon will not
> be able to leave you and I am told that I have
> been writing for one quarter of an hour before
> visitors I did not even see enter my bedroom.
> Farewell, farewell, tell yourself everything I am
> thinking—that will make you happier than all
> you have just read. Tell me of your return and,
> in the name of God, write me often. It is the
> greatest pleasure you could give me and one
> that you cannot refuse.

In these letters, Adrienne appears to have neglected the theatre entirely, even though her health had taken no serious turns that would prevent her from performing. Indeed, she still was the reigning queen of the French stage. Aside from the great classic tragedies, in 1725 she played Voltaire's *Hérode et Mariamne*, the revised version of his ill-fated *Mariamne* of the previous season.

What a rare treat for the public when, on April 10, the Comédie-Française performed this drama with Adrienne in the title role, and Duclos as Salomé. The two, each of very different talent, had their partisans and enemies. Naturally, the admirers of one were oblivious to the qualities of the other, and it is not hard to imagine the atmosphere of the theatre that evening. Each artist, encouraged by the bravos of her friends and by the hope of triumphing over her rival, put forth her greatest effort. Voltaire's play itself must surely have derived much benefit from this rivalry. For it was a retelling of the biblical tale of Herod, his queen, and his step-daughter, with all the complicated *coups de théâtre, jeux de scène*, and *quiproquo* which the fashion of the theatre then demanded. The affected style of a Duclos could not much longer resist comparison with the natural acting style of Adrienne. Admirers of Salomé became rare, and those of Mariamne more numerous. Voltaire tells us that Adrienne "buried her rival," and that Queen Marie Leszinska, after seeing both actresses perform at Fontainebleau, publicly expressed her preference for the younger woman.

The defeat of the partisans of the old school of declamation was not being brought about without furious resistance. Adrienne may well have had the public on her side, but this did not prevent endless persecution by her rivals. Heading the opposition were, naturally, Desmares and Duclos who, early in Adrienne's career, and once her success was evident to them, lost no time in seeking out younger and more attractive young women to oppose her success.

One of these was Mademoiselle Aubert who made her debut several months after Adrienne's. But it was not until the 1721–22 season that Mlle Aubert finally succeeded—doubtlessly with the prodding of Desmares and Duclos—to provoke Adrienne to the point of refusing to perform with her:

December 29, 1721

> I beg the Company not to count on me for Thursday's *Britannicus* if Mlle Aubert is to play Agrippine. I would be very happy if Mlle Dangeville would be good enough to play Junie. But nothing will determine me to ignore my resolve not to perform with Mlle Aubert.

The Assembly turned the matter over to the First Gentleman of the King's Chamber because "if such things were allowed to continue, we would not be able to perform at all." It is not clear how the matter was settled. The performance of *Britannicus* was cancelled for that Thursday, but the records show that the following Friday, January 2, both actresses appeared together in *Colin-Maillard*, a short comedy by Dancourt. Supporting Desmares and Duclos was the entire Quinault clan, thus giving those opposed to Adrienne a majority at the voting assemblies of the acting troupe. This formidable group lost no opportunity to vote for the imposition of numerous small fines upon Adrienne for infractions of various rules. The registers of the Comédie-Française are filled with this kind of petty notation:

> Mlle Lecouvreur is fined for tardiness, twice in the performance of *Rhadamiste*, twice during rehearsals of the *Foire de Bezons*, for tardiness in the performance of *Horaces*.

On occasion, the assembly was reluctantly obliged to recognize Adrienne's benefit to the Company and forced to decide that she would be "exempt from contributing to the pension fund in consideration of her usefulness to the troupe." On another occasion, both she and Mlle Duclos were voted extra dividends to be placed in escrow: "One-half of 5 quarter-dividends in consideration of the preciseness of their duties and their extraordinary expenses."

At times an authority higher than her colleagues had to be called upon to protect her from their vicious attacks: "May 1, 1725: 100 *livres* to be deducted from Mlle de Seine's share for having abused Mlle Lecouvreur; she is further warned that she will be dismissed from the troupe in case of any repetition of her act." Whatever

Mlle de Seine had done to Adrienne may have been no worse than another actor's discovery that an anagram for Lecouvreur is *couleuvre* (snake). But her enemies did go much further than that. On September 27, 1723, Philippe Poisson, a retired member of the troupe and sometime author, presented his former colleagues with a comedy in one act entitled *The New Actress*. Nothing more than a colorless satire of Adrienne's acting style and private life, the play was read and mimed before the troupe by the elder Quinault, who so amused his audience that the play was at once accepted for a trial performance. As it turned out, its only harm was in its intent. By calling upon her superiors, Adrienne was able to have the performance cancelled. The author had made no pretense at subtlety in his allusion to Adrienne:

> *De fables, de romans, sa chambre est toute
>   pleine:*
> *Sans cesse elle s'habille en princesse
>   romaine . . .*
> *Vous pouvez acheter ce nouveau régiment,*
> *Monsieur: j'en ai pour vous obtenu l'agrément*
> *Venez la voir en foule, elle aime le grand
>   monde*

> Her bedchamber is encumbered with fables
>   and novels,
> she dresses endlessly like a Roman queen . . .
> You may buy this new regiment, Monsieur:
> I have obtained consent for you.
> Crowd in to see her, she loves high society

This last is an obvious allusion to her relationship with Maurice de Saxe.

128

MAURICE DE SAXE

In the late summer and early fall, the troupe would be called upon to make its annual trip to Fontainebleau which, in 1725, began on August 31 and continued until November 26. Here, in the beautiful surroundings of the sixteenth-century palace, Adrienne was charmed by reflections of former moments of happiness with Maurice and by the anticipation of his imminent return:

Fontainebleau, Friday evening,
August 31, 1725.

I arrived about one hour ago and have had more trunks and packages unpacked than would be needed to supply your entire regiment. How cumbersome women are with all the equipment which is thought necessary for them! If it weren't for that, I would have written to you one hour earlier and consequently would have written more and would express more keenly my feelings for you; for, whatever one might say, the mind and the heart feel the effects of the body's hard labor. Weak as I am, I look forward to a happy stay here: having arrived under better auspices than last year, I find the forest more beautiful and my apartment admirable. I do not at all feel that sadness that cost me so much during last year's stay. You will soon see that I flatter myself that you love me and are happy with me. I will see you every day and even more often than in Paris; and this thought brings me a joy I cannot express. Everyone is pleased to be here as a spectator of the festivities, and I am exceedingly delighted at being able to tell you more often and more lovingly that I love you with all my heart.

My love for you has doubled on arriving here. The sight of a certain rock has warmed me. The

fact that we will not be the happiest lovers at
this Court is not because of me. That pleasure
belongs to the master and mistress [Louis XV
and Marie Leszinska, who were to be married
here on September 5] as young and as novice
as they are . . .

Great preparations are being made for the
arrival of the Queen. The entire *parterre* of the
Tibre is scaffolded and filled with machinery
for the fireworks and illuminations. But still, we
will be happier than they if you wish it.
Goodnight, my love, I am going to sleep, or
rather will I think of you.

At the marriage of the King and Marie Leszinska, the
most brilliant assemblage in the world filled the Château
de Fontainebleau. Voltaire wrote that there was a "noise,
clashing, press of people, and frightening tumult."
Maréchal Villars and the Comte d'Argenson accompanied
the Queen around the garden "speaking to her of affairs
of state in the shade of the same trees that had already
witnessed similar conversations between Henri IV and
Sully." As for the illuminations Adrienne mentions, these,
according to one witness, were rather unsuccessful: "A
strong wind extinguished the torches as soon as they were
lit." Voltaire reported that "after supper there were fireworks with many fuses and slight invention." The great
hall of the *Belle Cheminée* was transformed into a theatre;
the Queen was very moved by Adrienne's performances
of Mariamne and Hortense. It was reported that "the
tears of Marie Leszinska were the success of Voltaire and
the triumph of the actress." Later on, Adrienne would
be able to attest to the kindness of the Queen whose

virtues, according to history, appear to have inspired de-
votion and respect. As Adrienne was to report to Maurice:

> The Queen has spoken of me with much
> kindness, and despite the presence of two
> princesses, she declared loudly that she
> preferred me. This caused much talk and it is
> said that I should be very happy over this.

We are not surprised when Adrienne adds:

> I am in fact happy at this moment, but it is
> because I have read your letter and have reason
> to flatter myself that you love me.

But now both Maurice and Adrienne were completely
involved in his expedition to the Polish feudal state, the
former province of Latvia on the Baltic Sea, known as
the Duchy of Courland.

When Maurice began to conceive the plan to have himself elected sovereign of the Duchy, Adrienne did not object too strongly. Whether because she had a vision of
herself as Duchess of Courland, or because she did not
wish to stand in the way of her lover's prodigious career,
she at first was content to give him the encouragement
he needed and did not hesitate to offer sound advice:

> The King could die [Maurice's father,
> Augustus II, born in Dresden in 1670, was to
> die—years later, in 1733]. You are very far from
> him; and since he has no thought of his own of
> establishing you in a manner worthy of you, then
> you must make him understand that he is
> obliged to do so. Do not think that there is
> generosity in asking nothing in such a case. Kings

131

want to be solicited, even pestered, and you
should know this better than I. To oblige him
to do you some good is to do him honor. Oh,
that I could speak with him or write him. My
zeal would not appear at all suspect, for
assuredly, I have only his glory and your
happiness in view. . . .

But now the great enterprise which was supposed to
elevate Maurice to that so shaky and coveted northern
throne was about to take form during the trips to Saxony
and Poland in 1724 and 1725. If Adrienne, whose de-
votion and, indeed, whose very fortune were going to
contribute to the struggle, ever dreamed of sharing an
ephemeral crown, her purpose would have been to reign
over a subjected lover rather than over a turbulent people. Not resisting the prospect of this double life, her
troubled thoughts followed the perilous cavalcade into
the desolate plains of those northern provinces whose
"ferocious manners" horrified her.

Chapter Seven

THE COURLAND AFFAIR
1726–1728

HE FLAT, SWAMPY land known as Courland is now part of the Soviet Socialist Republic of Latvia. It is still inhabited in great part by the remains of a Wendish tribe who resisted the spread of Christianity for many years. Their descendants, the Letts and Kurs, were conquered in the early thirteenth century by the Livonian Knights, who succeeded in converting them and who amalgamated with the Order of Teutonic Knights in 1237. In 1561, to secure protection against the growing power of the Moscovites, the Teutonic Knights accepted the suzerainty of Catholic Poland, although they themselves had lately turned Protestant. The Teutonic Order's Grand Master, Gotthard Kettler, thus became the first Duke of Courland and founded a dynasty which was still governing the country when Maurice was born.

But in 1711, the dynasty was drawing to a close. Duke Frederick William, the husband of Anna Ivanovna, Peter the Great's niece, had died, leaving the succession to his uncle Ferdinand, who had aged beyond any possibility of providing himself with a future heir. There was no dearth of candidates, however, for the ducal crown which would become available upon Duke Ferdinand's death.

133

There was the Hereditary Prince of Hesse-Cassel, the Margrave Albert of Brandenburg, and Prince Menchikov, that famous adventurer of low birth whom imperial favor had elevated to the rank of chief adviser to Czar Peter. The Duchy's geographical position between four conflicting powers—Poland, Sweden, Russia, and Prussia— made its future a question of real international importance.

The nobles of Courland had a right to elect a successor to their sovereign, even during his lifetime. But their choice was subject to the consent of their suzerain, the King of Poland, Maurice's father. If no choice were made, then the Duchy would be incorporated into the Republic of Poland.

Although Poland had a king, this function was not hereditary. The king was elected by the Polish Diet, and kept his rights and privileges as long as he protected those of the Polish nobility. Augustus had already been deposed once in favor of King Stanislas (future father of the Queen of France), and he was always careful not to endanger his second chance. Since the Diet of Courland could not agree on a successor, they made it known that a Saxon prince, son of their liege lord of Poland, might very well fit the position.

Augustus had seriously considered Maurice for the dukedom rather than let it lapse to Poland. But he feared an alliance between the Sweden of Charles XII and Russia, whose purpose would be to re-establish Stanislas on the Polish throne. He therefore committed himself to the election of the Margrave of Brandenburg, who would then marry Anna Ivanovna, the Duchess of Courland. After Charles XII's death in 1718, Augustus abandoned this plan leaving the way clear for the ambitions of Count von Flemming, whom Voltaire called "the most defiant of men and one whom the neighboring powers most distrusted." This man was a favorite of Augustus, and was also his minister. But he was also the enemy of Maurice, who later was to describe him as "a brave and tireless worker, with exaggerated ambition, the most evil man under heaven, with little affection for honest men, an implacable enemy . . . as brutal as a drayhorse, slightly mad, and given to fantasy." But when faced with the necessity of betraying Augustus and uncertain of Czar Peter's support, Flemming did not press for his own advancement. As Voltaire put it, he "remained faithful to his benefactor," King Augustus.

Augustus needed only the invitation of Empress Catherine to "choose a prince of his house to be established upon the throne of Courland." Finally he ordered Maurice to make plans for gaining success in this affair—not so easy a matter considering the number of adversaries. The King wished only to please Russia, but Maurice was gratified at receiving his father's protection, even if it had come about in a rather devious way.

François Lefort, Saxony's envoy to Russia, sent for Maurice who was just burning for new adventure. He left for St. Petersburg in great haste. Lefort intended to arrange a marriage for Maurice with the highly cooperative Anna Ivanovna, who had privately stated that she was indeed interested in the much talked-about son of Augustus. But when he arrived at the Russian court, Maurice learned that Lefort had changed his plans. In place of the niece of the Czar of Russia, Lefort would now substitute her cousin, none other than the daughter

135

of Peter the Great, Elizabeth Petrovna. Lefort wrote to Flemming:

> Princess Elizabeth is not an impossible prize:
> with the aid of the strongbox, the prize is ours.
> The Duchess of Courland will have a price as
> well, but not so high.

As for the Empress Catherine, she would have for her son-in-law none other but Maurice.

But Maurice was not interested in either of these royal ladies, each of whom one day in her turn would reign over all the Russias. If he was to wear the ducal crown, he would have it for either his political ability or his talent at waging war.

On his return to Warsaw, Maurice was greeted by the most important members of Courland's nobility, who informed him that despite Flemming's threats, on April 25, 1726, their council of ministers had agreed to Maurice's election as Duke-Coadjutor, a title he would hold while the old Duke Ferdinand still lived. Maurice was to leave Warsaw immediately for Courland and St. Petersburg on the pretext of claiming restitution of the Moen Islands, his mother's estate in Estonia. But on May 21, King Augustus had a change of heart—largely due to a formal protest lodged by Polish Chancellor Szembek who, speaking for the Polish nobility, was doubtlessly upset at the thwarting of plans for the division of Courland once it lapsed to Poland and suspicious of the Saxon King's scheme for the aggrandizement of his own family. When Maurice, booted and spurred, received notification of his royal father's wish that he remain in Warsaw, he is alleged to have remarked: "Whoever catches me will have to be a champion runner." Flemming, of course, was quite concerned over the real possibility the Poles would send him and King Augustus packing back to Saxony once again.

On May 28, Maurice's half-brother, the Prince-Royal, wrote him:

> I am told that you intend to lead a company of
> noblemen in an effort to convince the others to
> take up arms; I must tell you that I have no faith
> in this and hasten to assure you in advance that
> you will not receive the King's assent. As for me,
> I agree with you that a noble death is preferable
> to a shameful life. I leave you to think about
> whether or not a noble death is possible in such
> an enterprise.

But Maurice had already made his decision:

> The sacrifice is ready in Courland. . . . If I am
> condemned by the King, I will be the victim.
> But I cannot betray those to whom I have given
> my word and be thus dishonored in the eyes of
> an entire country which has put its confidence
> in me. . . . If it means fighting only the Poles,
> you will shortly see me heading an army to
> oppose them. . . . On the enclosed paper I have
> set down the traditional rights of the nobles of
> Courland in the election of a duke, and I beg
> you to read it with attention. If this is to be a
> war of documents, then I will send you others;
> and I assure you, Monseigneur, that I do not fear
> the Republic [of Poland] in either respect.

Maurice, not certain of the continued support of Russia, who might force a meeting of the Estates-General of Courland to elect another, felt inclined to hurry things along. He was unanimously elected Duke-Successor on

May 28th, and was thus able to foil the mission of Prince Dolgorouki who had appeared in Mittau, Courland's capital, with orders to prevent the election. A more formidable opponent next appeared in the person of Prince Menchikov. Having hurried to Mittau from St. Petersburg, he begged, threatened, offered enormous sums of money, and placed his troops on Courland's frontiers, but to no avail. In the ten days since Maurice's arrival at Mittau, the enthusiasm of Courland's nobles grew by leaps and bounds: "They are unflinching," Maurice wrote to his mother. "They have sworn to renew in my service the heroism of their ancestors, the Knights of the Teutonic Order. Ah! rest assured that here there are brave men who love me with all their souls."

The women were no less ardent. One of Maurice's biographers reported that from one end of Europe to the other, there was an entire legion of women who exhibited passionate interest in Maurice's success:

> There is a mixture of rank as well as affection:
> a mother, an emperor's daughter, great ladies of
> Dresden, Warsaw, Mittau, Riga, and an actress.

In addition to the two Russian princesses, those ever-ready fiancées, there were Maurice's half-sisters, Countess Ruthowska, Countess de Cosel, who became the Countess von Friesen, and Countess Orzelska, who was to marry Prince von Holstein in 1731. Orzelska wrote to her brother:

> Rest assured, my dear brother, that I shall do all
> possible for your happiness. I have spoken in
> your favor to the King and I dare say that he

138

> thinks well of you and is not angry. As for the
> devil [Flemming] I have heard nothing; he would
> not dare speak too loudly, you have too many
> friends around here. . . .

Following Maurice's official election, Menchikov advanced with an army of 12,000 Russians and quickly placed Maurice's headquarters under siege. On July 20, 1726, Maurice wrote to his brother-in-law Count von Friesen: "I am preparing for an alert tonight." But by daybreak, the Empress Catherine, furious that Menchikov had taken matters into his own hands, had already ordered him to break camp. Shortly after his return to Russia, the continuation of his high-handed policies in opposition to the wishes of the Empress (who had been his mistress before Peter the Great took her from his house, and whom he helped raise to the throne on Peter's death), brought about his final disgrace. At the accession of Peter II in 1727, he was brusquely dismissed and exiled to Siberia, where he died two years later.

The Poles' only interest, however, was to see Courland returned to their Republic so that it could be divided into palatinates and offered up to the nobles. And they were not disarming. Several European courts, surprised by Maurice's success, were about to send ambassadors to the Polish Diet at Grodno with the intention of undermining its work. King Augustus grew more frightened as everything seemed to combine to destroy Maurice's election. He officially declared himself against Maurice and joined forces with his Polish subjects. On October 15 he wrote to Maurice informing him that he had been declared an enemy of the Republic and that there was a price on his head. Troops would be sent to force the nobles of Courland to renounce the election and to accept incorporation with Poland in accordance with the constitution which the King was obliged to support. Here is Maurice's answer:

> Sire,
>
> It grieves me to disobey Your Majesty, but I no longer belong to myself, and I can do nothing without the consent of the nobles of Courland. I appeal this situation to Your Majesty's heart. If I am not already condemned, I will give myself up to whatever Fortune may decree.

On November 15 he wrote to Count von Friesen:

> Well, my dear Count, here I am condemned, a price on my head! God have mercy on me if I am caught. I suppose I now can expect as much protection as a wolf. . . . Ah, gentlemen of the Senate and of the Republic, you will pay for Flemming's stupidity and you will witness some great events. So you wish me to take up arms? So be it! This I will do; and so long as I am able to hold a sword, I will use it to destroy you. This is where, my dear Count, one must either be victorious or die. I would begin had I only 100 men, and when they fall I would seek others, and I will continue as long as there is a breath in my body. . . .

Aurora von Königsmark was living out her last years as the Abbesse-Coadjutor at Quedlinburg, where she avidly followed her son's predicament. She was sick with worry, but strengthened by a mother's pride when Maurice wrote:

> Give me a free hand, Madame, you will see the
> old Königsmark come alive under your eyes,
> the one who held Germany's armies in check!

She had sold the remains of her former opulence for Maurice's cause. What further aid could Maurice hope for from Maria-Aurora, whom Voltaire later described as:

> That woman, famous for her mind and beauty,
> more capable than any minister of state of
> making a successful negotiation.

But Maurice did need financial support, and for this he turned to his friends in France. The first to respond was Adrienne. Pawning her diamonds, silverplate, and carriages, she was able to raise the sum of 40,000 *livres*, about 200,000 dollars, a considerable sum even today. Now her thoughts were devoted entirely to the plight of her lover who "was running furious dangers and chancing unforeseen accidents:"

December 31, 1726.

> After not hearing from you for a very long
> time, I suddenly received nine packets in two
> days and have been receiving letters twice a
> week regularly. When one considers all the
> details in this affair, it is impossible not to be
> completely impatient with the father; his conduct
> is as blameful and inconceivable as yours is
> worthy and honorable in the midst of all
> reverses. But what can be done against the
> strength and shameful weakness of a king who
> allows himself to be governed by the cruelest
> enemy of his glory, a man who hates the son of

141

whom he is not worthy. Through hate, envy and
self-interest, they have combined their forces
against such a fine undertaking. Now your
adversaries are continuing with double the
energy since your condemnation was voted by
the Diet and signed by the King. Is it possible to
imagine the signing of an act putting a price on
that head—a father, for a noble project which he
had at first approved and which would certainly
be useful to him one day. The rise of Flemming
is unsurmountable, or rather, there is no more
humanity or reason in that soul. All this is mingled
with indescribable circumstances which cause
one to be even more attached to you and totally
impatient (to use an understatement) with the
one who shows so much weakness . . .

The threatened subjects are holding out well,
but what will they do against two powerful
kingdoms and a great empire? The Prussians
are united with the Russians, and both have thus
far kept out of it. But we must not be deceived.
I believe the battle is lost.

It is evident that Adrienne had kept fully abreast of the
proceedings. One is even surprised at the great detail
and historical accuracy of her information:

England promised aid which she no longer
intends to give; and, as a pretext, she insists that
she does not wish to be contrary to King
Augustus who has declared himself diametrically
opposed to the confirmation of the election.
Barricades have been thrown up in the capital
[Mittau] and one cannot abandon people who
are willing to perish to defend their right and
their choice. But if they persist they will be torn
to pieces; they will be attacked on all sides as

soon as the fighting begins. This is what I see.
The entire affair perfectly resembles a novel,
and I am dying for fear of approaching the
catastrophe. In truth, that would be horrible, and
I cannot describe the extent of my torment.

The palaceless and revenueless Duke with a force of 100 men, forty of whom were already casualties, made an effort to overcome his boredom in the dismal capital. A Swedish nobleman, writing to Aurora von Königsmark, informed her that Maurice had been reduced to spending most of his day in bed reading *Don Quixote*. His imagination was not at rest, however. His plans, always of vast proportion and great risk, included offering England a port in Courland on the Baltic Sea. This detail had to be abandoned after threats by the great powers. As pointed out by Adrienne, England took the diplomatic way out.

At this point Adrienne actually believed that once rid of all thoughts of the ducal crown, Maurice would depart for Paris and eventually marry her. Indeed, in the following letter, she states the uselessness of his cause, advises Maurice to obtain the King's pardon and to regain his favor, and all but begs him to renounce the hope of an odious crown which can be nothing more than an obstacle to their happiness:

dated 1726

Oh, my dear Count, why are you not here?
The sight of you would forestall any misfortune
with which I might be threatened. I would not
die before you, but would live in happiness if
you loved me as you once did. Do you

143

remember? Absence and a thousand new
interests have by now erased from your soul
those feelings which control my joy and sorrow,
my hope and fear. What can you not read in my
soul from where you are? or rather, why are you
not here? Speak to me of your return, as distant
as it might be. If only you could bring that
moment closer, if only you could desire it as I
do. It is my heart that speaks; it was never more
yours and will never belong to anyone else. If
you love me and have some wish that my health
improve, even though you cannot return sooner,
at least write to me often and write long letters.
Perhaps there is still something in me that can
enflame your desire. . . .

Sacrifice, travel, anything you could desire, I
will never weigh in the balance. But write to me,
tell me what you are doing, your pleasures, your
health. . . . At least I will then be sure that for
a short time you have thought of me. This will be
the wages of your love which will be precious to
me and which will keep me alive. . . .

Take advantage of the time; see to your
enemies; move those who are attached to you;
and don't waste your time in useless resentment.
Remember that dissimulation is permitted and
even necessary to persons of your birth and that
you could not better avenge yourself than by
acquiring respect, and, I dare say, fortune has
much to do with it. It is the shame of the human
race, but this does not prevent it from being so.
Besides, this trickery which I do advise you to
engage in can do you no harm where more
highly born souls than you are concerned, and
for the King's glory it is necessary. It is in spite
of myself that I push you to flatter him into doing

well by you; you will need more time to convince
him and this means only that you will have less
time for me. Once this is accomplished you will
be less to my taste, for I would love you a
thousand times more as a simple resident of
Daumartin than if you possessed all the crowns
in the world. However, I would risk my life a
thousand times over to procure for you an
establishment worthy of you. I love you for
yourself, and you will never be loved more
perfectly.

Why can I not speak to your King? He would
pay no attention to my entreatments nor to the
extent your interests and his glory move me.
But if, through me, he grasped all your worth,
he would never allow you to return to Paris.
The tiny house at Daumartin appears even more
beautiful than all the world's courts. There we
are alone, free and happy. There no intrigue
occupies our minds; your dogs are your only
courtiers and love our only concern. Is there
anything in life sweeter? Isn't life too short to
neglect the greatest good in the world? You
know the answer to this question better than any
King, for never has a king been loved as you
have.

Adieu, my dear Count and Lord, if I followed
my inclination, I would never stop writing to
you. I would kiss the hand and embrace the
knees of Madame la Comtesse de Königsmark.
But I have no more paper.

Adrienne.

At the end of April of 1727, Maurice was in Paris attempting to interest Cardinal de Fleury in his behalf and
was to leave without success after several weeks. During

this short stay Adrienne wrote happy messages to Maurice as he went about his business:

> . . . Last night you were the topic of
> conversation. In the little guessing games we
> played, it was revealed that all my desires, at every
> instant, concerned you. I was questioned as to
> why you do not spend more time at Court. If
> you were seen there more often, I could avoid
> this kind of discussion and would thus have much
> pleasure. . . . It would be very thoughtful of
> you to arrive on Tuesday early. In the meantime,
> think of me, but I fear that your hunting will
> roughen your tenderness for me. . . . This
> evening I could have no ill thoughts concerning
> anyone. My blood tingles and I have my health.
> These are surely two important points. I love
> you and I am easily vanquishing my enemies
> without being so unfortunate as to hate them,
> which indeed would be a great torment.

Adrienne's "enemies" had lately gained new support with the defection to their side of her neighbor and long-time intimate friend, the Abbé d'Amfreville, a close associate of the Duc de Bouillon. The exact nature of this affair is not clear; but we do know, from an undated letter to the Marquis de Rochemore, that Adrienne was deeply hurt by the Abbé's apparent treason:

> I am overcome with anger and sorrow, my
> dear R. . . . I was bathed in tears the whole
> night through. Perhaps this is foolishness since
> I have done nothing to reproach; but I cannot
> bear unmerited injustice. All that disillisions me
> with regard to friendship drives me to despair. I
> have more courage where love is concerned since

it is involuntary. I know its effects as well as the
wisdom of removing oneself from it at an early
stage, and especially of preparing oneself for its
inconstancies when one least suspects them. In
this respect my misfortunes and experience have
furnished matter for reflection for my entire life.
But while arming myself against it through
precaution and reason, I have always been
careful to enrich friendship with the left-overs
of love, so that each year, day, and moment, if it
is possible, have only strengthened in me the
desire for friends, to preserve them, and to merit
their respect.

You know with what confidence I treat those
I have chosen and especially the honesty of my
conduct. I have hidden nothing from you.
However, I am suspected and accused, and even
worse, they would convict me without the
opportunity to defend myself; and if by chance
I should learn and uncover what is transpiring,
I would be victimized by the most horrible
calumny that ever was by a man who for ten
years has called himself my friend. I am told not
to tell you; I respect and love the one who has
given me this advice; but I cannot hold it in; I
am too stunned, too wounded, and too frightened
for the future not to give vent to my feelings at
least with you. I need advice. A man capable of
this treachery could very well think up others,
and what most upsets me is the need for
concealment. It is natural to cry out against
perfidy and I would prefer to pardon it than be
obliged to constrain both my sorrow and my
resentment.

They try to tell me that this is his way of
thinking, that he has no desire to wrong me, as

if I were like any woman. I cannot go along with
this idea. That certainly is not the language he
was accustomed to use for ten years, and that
cannot be the reward for my great care to please
him and to gain his respect at least according to
my merit. In the end, what can one do other than
mortally wounding me where I am most sensitive?
I could destroy the lie in an instant. But how can
I console myself with the intention of the slander?
This is a man who must know me and who
should love me. This is more than a nasty word
said in passing; it took the form of a confidence
made in detail before a man who has only
friendship for me, a friendship dearer to me than
all the passion in the world, whose respect is
more precious than life, and whose society I
need more than all the fortune in the universe. It
is before him that I am painted as false and
contemptible. No matter what he says, they
bear witness to my alleged crime.

Evidently it is Rochemore himself whom Adrienne's
enemies wish to convince of her "crime":

Oh my God! what will we do since I am advised
that you should not know and I want to tell you
without offending the one who forbids it. It is
my secret, it is I who am oppressed on all sides.
It could go further and I would be relieved to
have counsel and a defender. It is thought that
perhaps you might explode in anger, which would
serve only to embitter minds and convince them
of the truthfulness of the slander whose authors
I have found out; but you must say nothing of
this. I know you are moved, but you must
maintain more composure than I have. . . . So
now I have a new and dangerous enemy who is

148

all the more so considering our friendship and closeness which appeared to be permanent, one who is bright and against whom I cannot stir up enough hate in order to take revenge or to silence him.

Here I am with my tears, the usual expedient for my misfortunes, and my dark thoughts, a sad remedy for evil, and they want me to hide this from you! You are precisely the one I can speak to. Who can better sympathize and judge? No, I do not have enough virtue to be capable of that effort. If I had followed my first inclination, I would have sent to you last evening thus avoiding an atrocious night. You would have consoled and advised me. For God's sake, R. . . . , do not abandon me and if possible, prove to me that friendship is not an illusion. If I am ever made to see that it is, I would want to die.

It is at this time in 1727 that Adrienne found it necessary to send her twenty-two-year-old sister, Marie-Marguerite to a convent:

To Monseigneur the Lieutenant-General of Police:

Adrienne Lecouvreur humbly begs your honor to be good enough to expedite the King's order for the reception of Marguerite Lecouvreur, her sister, into the community of the Convent of Saint-Michel, rue des Postes, Faubourg Saint-Marceau, where she has arranged with the Mother Superior to pay her sister's pension. She asks this favor for reasons which will be explained to you by your Secretary, Monsieur Rossignol.

149

We know that Marie-Marguerite had convinced Adrienne's neighbors that she had been locked in a third-floor room and fed on bread and water. This perhaps may explain, in part, the reason why her long-time friend and neighbor, the Abbé d'Amfreville, suddenly broke with her. It may be the very calumny she referred to in the above letter. But she soon gained the upper hand and was able to devote herself entirely to Maurice during his short mission to Paris—where he did not stay more than a month.

He was back in Germany in June, and at Pillnitz had a conversation with his father. The interview passed off satisfactorily, not a word being said about Courland. He and his small company then went to Mittau, where the situation had changed for the worse. In Warsaw, the entire Courland delegation had been thrown into prison and a Polish army was moving toward the border. But, worst of all, Catherine of Russia was dead, leaving Maurice without his most powerful protector. Menchikov, who had lately been controlled by the Empress, used the interim before the crowning of young Czar Peter II to assume direction of affairs in Russia. He immediately sent an army to Courland to prevent its being annexed by the Poles.

Now pursued by two armies and finally abandoned by the Courlanders, Maurice took refuge on an island in the middle of Lake Ursmaiten or Asmeyden, alone with his guards and several recruits from the Netherlands. There were 12 officers, 104 infantrymen, 98 dragoons, and 33 servants. The Russian troops, having crossed the Duna, were now in Courland. On August 12, 1727, General Lacy presented himself to Maurice in the name of the

Czar and stated that he had the order to attack. The next morning, with the Russian troops on the banks of the lake and the Poles certain to appear at any moment, Maurice got the Russians to agree to his retirement to the Prussian port of Nemel, accompanied by several officers.

Once there he learned of the formal conclusion of his great adventure. On August 26 the Polish commissioners, escorted by 500 dragoons, entered Mittau. The Russians withdrew, but their commander hinted that he would tolerate no harsh proceedings against the Courlanders, whose nobles immediately rescinded the decree of June 28, 1726. Menchikov's fall from power brought about no reversal of Russia's policy concerning Courland. Thus ended, in unheroic fashion, Maurice's bid for the ducal crown of Courland.

Adrienne received the news of the outcome with joy. But her happiness was soon dispelled when he wrote to her from Frankfort to tell her that he was on his way to Breslau. It was evident that he was as busy as ever with schemes for his own advancement. Her hopes for his definitive return to Paris were shattered:

Paris, December 5, 1727.

I have finally received your letter dated in Frankfort which took much longer to reach me than the others. I pity you with all my heart for the terrible trials you are undergoing, but they cannot be so bad since you do not seem to be tiring of them. Your new plans for next year seem very courageous, but they absolutely nullify mine, and I cannot hide this from you. You tell me that you intend to be here for three months, as if the knowledge of this should be a

151

complete delight. What happiness, you say! I
thought you were returning for good. Now it is
clear that you wish to spend your life amidst the
horrors that come from ambition . . . and, come
what may, I can no longer hope for happiness.

It is not fitting that I make demands of you,
and I am incapable of even wishing for a single
sacrifice on your part; but I cannot tolerate the
idea of eternally living as I do, always fearing for
the present and never certain of the future. For
two years of suffering, you well know that there
was never a love more alive or a more exacting
faithfulness. If your plans had an end, whether
good or bad, I would make my decision and wait
with courage; but the uncertainty takes away all
hope and makes me wish that I had never loved
you, for I lead a detestable life, one that is
assuredly unbearable for everyone else. I have
lived in fear and bitterness for two years; when I
thought you were returning for good, I looked
upon those two years as a pleasure. Now that I
see no end to your plans, those two years appear
as a torture.

It would be comforting to be able to uphold
my encouragement and support, but I have never
done anything except through the natural
movement of my heart, which no longer inspires
either patience or courage in me. Your plan to
return disgusts me. I see it in a completely
different light. You have no support, you deal
only with traitors, and you act for weak and
uncertain people who have failed you; I do not
forgive them for not having loved you in every
possible way. You are deceived and flattered
and you are perishing in all this in spite of your
courage. I am exhausted and have no more

152

courage; I would almost prefer not to see you again than to see you only to lose you. My situation is horrible because I must reproach myself for what I am saying. I think you still love me although your love for glory is stronger. I would never forgive myself if I destroyed that sentiment in you because you would love me less for it and would hold me suspect for having denied your happiness. You are certain to find a hundred mistresses, but glory might never again come your way. And I, spending my life in fear and aging in boredom, what will there be for me when your adventures are at an end? A heart, tired of the gratitude you think you owe me, and of the illnesses brought on by time, or the despair of seeing you perish through treachery or some stroke of fortune. . . .

Here some say, "She is mad"; others "she is fooling us and is not faithful." I do not even know whether you still believe that, but the knowledge that you do could excuse everything. You are more suspicious than anyone, and if it is ever to your interest to doubt my faithfulness, you will certainly never weigh the question, and I would lose everything—your heart and the price of my constancy. Such are men. All this is human. How angry I am with myself for having been born so different from so many others! I do not believe I am the only woman capable of thinking in this way, but I do hold that it is a misfortune, especially when one is attached to someone filled with ambition. This is a fault I prefer to many others, for, as you well know, I have a secret and avid liking for real valor and, of course, glory, but like neither when pushed to the extreme or when they cause my unhappiness. . . . If the Courlanders had helped

153

you before the Russian intervention, you would not be where you are. The Polish made most of this affair, and the Courlanders were wrong to bend so quickly; I hold them as subjugated people and no longer love them.

All I have is pity for them. That is enough for people who failed you when you sacrificed yourself for them. I can do no less than this for a people who chose you although that choice caused me to suffer. Finally, there is no further hope for anything that might make me support what you plan to do. Farewell, I have nothing more to say and I do not know how I could have written this much, given the terrible mood I am in.

But Maurice lingered on at Breslau. If he could not be a duke, there still seemed to be no reason why he should not become a prince-consort or climb to an imperial throne behind a wife. Through the efforts of the un-daunted ambassador Lefort, he made a final assault upon the hand of Princess Elizabeth. After a series of offers and counter-offers, he became aware of the lustful history of the young princess whose previous lovers had, one by one, been banished to Siberia or met mysterious ends. Eventually, Lefort wrote to his Court reporting the irregular conduct of the daughter of Peter the Great, whom he no longer considered a fitting wife for Maurice. Adrienne, hearing of his revived interest in Elizabeth, wrote wearily to a friend: "I do not believe it will come off, not that I am dissuading him or that I flatter myself. I do my duty, that's all." If Maurice had dreams of being the Czar of Russia, he missed the chance twice: in 1730 Anna Ivanovna, dowager duchess of Courland, became

Empress of All the Russias, and twelve years later her cousin, naughty Princess Elizabeth, was the wearer of the imperial crown.

But another rumor stung Adrienne into a wrath. Flemming had died in April 1728, only six weeks after Aurora von Königsmark. His widow, a Radziwill princess, was reputed to be worth seven million *livres*. Why not avenge his old enemy by marrying his widow? But there is no proof that Maurice ever considered the marriage.

At last, on October 23, 1728, a courier informed Adrienne that Maurice's coach had broken down within thirty leagues of Paris. "We have sent out a chaise," wrote Adrienne, "he should be here this evening."

Life was less than blissful for the reunited couple. Maurice soon grew tired of the sad and jealous nature of his faithful mistress. The Duchesse de Bouillon, who had found him pleasing, invited both Adrienne and Maurice to her country house at Pontoise, during Easter of 1729, where Adrienne was received *en reine*. Some believe that it was during this visit that the Duchesse conceived the idea of doing away with Maurice's constant companion.

Chapter Eight

THE DUCHESSE AND
The Abbé
1729–1730

*ADAME DE BOUILLON is capricious, violent, headstrong, and excessively amorous; her tastes extend from princes of the blood all the way down to actors. Last month she took a fancy to the Comte de Saxe, who certainly has none for her. This is not because he prides himself on being faithful to Lecouvreur who has been his true inclination for some time, for he has not let this passion interfere with a thousand passing fancies. But he was neither flattered nor curious to respond to the overtures of Madame de Bouillon who was outraged at seeing her charms scorned and who had no doubt that Lecouvreur was the obstacle to the passion which the count should naturally have for her.*

The author of this portrait was Charlotte-Elisabeth Aïssé (originally Haydée) who was born somewhere in Turkey around 1694. At the age of four years she was purchased for 1500 *livres* in the slave market at Constantinople by Baron Charles de Ferriol, ambassador of France. He took her back to Paris, planning to raise her as a lady of quality so that he would have an appropriate concubine in his old age. But like Arnolphe, his fictional counterpart

157

in Molière's *Ecole des femmes*, his ambition was never fulfilled—he soon had to return to Constantinople where he eventually died, not before leaving little Aïssé in the care of his brother, Augustin de Ferriol, who raised her as one of his own children. We cannot ignore Aïssé's advantageous position as the adopted daughter of the Ferriol family which placed her in close contact with her foster brother, d'Argental. Her portrait of the Duchesse de Bouillon appears to be faithful to general opinion.

At a time when it caused no astonishment for ladies of rank to indulge their amorous whims, the young Duchesse de Bouillon's outrages finally wore down the public's indulgence. Born Louise-Henriette-Françoise de Lorraine, this woman was the fourth wife of the old Duc de Bouillon, forty years her senior, and head of one of France's most illustrious names, the house of La Tour d'Auvergne. She was also extremely beautiful, at least so we are told: "Tall, neither fat nor thin, oval face, high forehead, large black eyes and brown hair; an outstanding mouth with vermillion lips; a large beauty-patch close to the right eye." Although she was the acknowledged mistress of the Comte de Clermont, she did have a taste for stage personalities, as Aïssé reported. At the Comédie-Française, her name had been linked with that of Quinault-Dufresne and the younger Grandval; at the Opéra she knew the singer Tribou. But if we may believe the memoires of a certain Abbé Aunillon Delaunay du Gué (one of her closest acquaintances, who appears to contradict Aïssé), Maurice de Saxe did all in his power to win the Duchesse's esteem—and that in order to ease Adrienne's suspicions, the Duchesse was very gracious to her

158

rival. Whichever is the correct version, the Duchesse was evidently aware that she had a strong opponent and Maurice was not one to ignore the advances of so beautiful a woman with so illustrious a name.

The following July, Adrienne was undoubtedly startled by a communication she received from an unknown person:

> Mademoiselle,
>   You will be surprised that a person you do not know is writing to you to beg you to be, tomorrow Monday, at five-thirty in the afternoon, on the grand terrace of the Luxembourg, where you will find a person who will explain things to you more fully; he will be recognized by this sign: an abbé who will strike his hat three times on approaching you.
> *Sunday, July 24, 1729.*

The next day, on the advice of friends, Adrienne went to the Luxembourg terrace, accompanied by Mlle de la Motte and an unnamed close friend, where they found an Abbé named Bouret. He told her that he felt obliged to warn her of a plot to poison her. She subsequently reported the affair to police-lieutenant Hérault who immediately arrested the Abbé.

The following information is pieced together from the answers Bouret gave to the examining police officers.

Siméon Bouret had been born in Metz in 1711, son of M. Bouret, treasurer of the Crown of France at Metz. Perhaps because the young Bouret was slightly misshapen, he sought refuge within the outer doors of the Church, taking those minor orders which gave him the title of *abbé*—which, in the eighteenth century, implied no particular priestly responsibilities. Whatever his responsibilities were, they did not interfere with the talent for miniature-painting in which he showed early promise. In December of 1728, his father brought him to Paris (they had made their first visit the year before) and left him there to continue to study his art.

The student shifted about from one petty hotel to another, little dreaming that every change of address would one day be traced by the police and recorded for the information of posterity. He was then 19 years old. Since he could not paint in the evening, and since he loved the theatre, he would attend the Comédie-Française almost every evening, where he soon made many acquaintances, both on and off the stage, and became a well-known figure. In fact, he would often be seen in the foyers of the theatre, coming from and going into various private boxes—and it may be that he was thus noticed by the Duchesse de Bouillon.

Shortly after this second arrival in Paris, he met a young man whom he had known the previous year at the painting academy of the Louvre. According to Bouret, the young man, named Périgord, was an excellent painter and was delighted at having found Bouret again. Périgord suggested that they go to celebrate at the Saint-Germain fair, and the two proceeded along the rue Dauphine, where Périgord recognized another friend, a young man of about 16 or 17, very tall, extremely handsome, dressed in livery, who was employed as a page by the Duchesse de Bouillon. Bouret's description makes it evident that he was deeply impressed with the boy's physical attributes:

> Tan complexion, very beautiful, light, chestnut hair, almost blond, worn in a bun or a queue, large black eyes, an aquiline nose, beautiful teeth and mouth, and red prominent lips.

The three continued on to the fair, where they browsed about an art dealer's shop. The page, noticing Bouret's interest in various paintings, asked whether the Abbé knew anything about art. Bouret replied that he could paint in miniature and hastened an offer to do a portrait of the page. The page was delighted and invited Bouret and Périgord to drink with him at a café. The three then had supper at a cabaret where the page paid the bill. They then parted—but not before agreeing to meet the next morning at the Hôtel de Bouillon, where Bouret would begin the page's portrait. The Hôtel de Bouillon was situated at the site of what is today No. 17, Quai Malaquais. This was just a stone's throw from the rue des Marais where Adrienne lived.

The next day the three breakfasted in the page's room. Once Périgord took his leave, Bouret started work on the miniature and devoted the following five or six days to this task. When the portrait was completed, it was framed inside the lid of a tortoise-shell tobacco box.

Having arranged with the page to go to the fair with him the next day, Bouret returned to the Hôtel de Bouillon to find the page awaiting him in the doorway. He had shown the portrait to the Duchesse, who found it exceedingly well executed. The page bade the Abbé enter and led him to an apartment where the Duchesse was waiting. Extremely polite and complimentary, she asked Bouret if he would not like to paint a miniature of her. Bouret replied that this would do him great honor and agreed to return in two days. Taking leave of the Duchesse, he accompanied the page to the fair.

Bouret's description of the Duchesse's apartment would appear to confirm the truth of his statement:

> After crossing two beautiful rooms, I entered her bedroom, gilded and paneled, without tapestries; there was a large sofa covered in green damask, chairs and stools covered in the same way, and above the sofa a single painting of a woman with Cupids and a faun; on the side, a drawn drape.

He began the portrait two days later and completed it in ten days. It was a bust slightly larger than a coin of 24 *sols*, which was to be attached to a bracelet.

During the course of her sittings, the Duchesse learned that the Abbé loved the theatre and asked him who were his favorite actors and actresses. To this he answered:

> As for actors, I see none better than the Quinaults; and as actresses, none better than Mademoiselle Lecouvreur and Duclos.

When the Duchesse inquired whether he knew Mademoiselle Lecouvreur personally, he replied that he knew her only from having seen her on the stage. The Duchesse then suggested that he arrange to meet Mademoiselle Lecouvreur or at least someone close to her: "Since you do not know her and she does not know you, you must render me a service which is to deliver to her a letter which I shall dictate to you." This she did, making it appear that the letter had been written by a prince of the blood who, declaring his love for Adrienne, insisted that she immediately give up the Comte de Saxe.

The next day, however, the Duchesse had a change of heart and requested the Abbé not to deliver the letter. She reminded the Abbé that since he could paint portraits, he could gain easy access to Adrienne's house. When Bouret protested, the Duchesse replied that the matter was quite simple—it had to do only with giving Adrienne a love philtre. During that afternoon's sitting, the Duchesse asked Bouret to meet her that night at the Tuileries gate.

Bouret was met at the gate by two masked men who escorted him to the Duchesse seated on a stone bench at the far end of the Pont Royal. The two men spoke of Bouret's earning a great deal of money, assuring him that he would not be asked to do anything criminal. His mission was simply to gain entrance to Adrienne's home and give her some lozenges whose effect would be to make her indifferent to the Comte de Saxe and cause her to love another. When the Abbé agreed, he was promised the sum of 6,000 *livres* plus an annual pension of 600 *livres*. The Duchesse, delighted at the Abbé's decision, attempted to glorify what he was about to do, not without reminding him of the reward: "You know what the gentlemen told you . . . she's a worthless girl; you must do it; it is even doing a service to the state. Besides, you can be certain of your reward." Bouret promised to do his best.

During the next sitting the Duchesse showed Bouret a print of Apollo and Isis unclothed. Proposing that Bouret draw her in the manner of the print, she stated that instead of Apollo she would wish to substitute a certain gentleman in the same condition of undress. Bouret objected, saying that he was not talented enough for that. The Duchesse replied that she would have been surprised if he were. The matter was dropped, and two days later the miniature of the Duchesse was completed. The Abbé was ordered not to return to the Hôtel before accomplishing the task that he had agreed to.

That evening, again at the Tuileries, the masked men insisted that the matter was now pressing and that, in any case, the Abbé risked nothing. They also warned him not to be surprised if the lozenges had a violent effect upon Mademoiselle Lecouvreur. "But, if they should cause her death?"

"—if that should happen, you still have nothing to fear; it is only a question of taking precautions. If anything goes wrong, we shall have a *chaise* ready to take you out of the country."

At this point, on the advice of the Capucin confessor who was his *confident*, the Abbé decided to warn Adrienne of the plot and wrote her his anonymous letter.

Adrienne, horrified by the knowledge that Bouret was being penalized for what she considered a sincere attempt to protect her, wrote to police-lieutenant Hérault on August 1, 1729:

> I have spoken with him and made him speak
> often and long, and he always answered with
> consistency and simplicity. It is not that I desire
> what he says to be true; I have a hundred times
> more reason to hope that he is mad. . . . But if
> he is innocent, think, Monsieur, of the interest I
> must have in his life, and how cruel the
> uncertainty is for me.

THE DUCHESSE AND THE ABBE

It would appear that Maurice did not believe the Abbé's story—which must have highly incensed Adrienne all the more because he continued his relationship with the Duchesse. On October 18, 1729, Maurice went to see Adrienne perform in *Phèdre*. As he seated himself in his accustomed place, Adrienne was speaking the words addressed to Hippolyte:

> ⚜ *Au défaut de ton bras, prête-moi ton épée!*

> ⚜ If I can't have your hand, lend me your
>   sword.

whereupon she seized Hippolyte's stage sword and flung it at Maurice, hitting him in the stomach. The following November 10, with Adrienne playing the same role, it was the turn of the Duchesse de Bouillon who received the unflaunting gaze of Theseus' Queen as she intoned those lines of vengence:

> ⚜ *Je ne suis point de ces femmes hardies*
>   *Qui, goûtant dans le crime une tranquille*
>   *paix,*
>   *Ont su se faire un front qui ne rougit jamais.*

> ⚜ I am not one of those bold women
>   Who, finding calm and peace in their crimes,
>   Are able to show a face which never blushes.

The audience, who knew what was going on, applauded wildly, which must have been quite upsetting to the Duchesse.

As Mademoiselle Aïssé later reported:

> Since then La Lecouvreur was on her guard.
> One day at the Comédie, after the performance

165

of the main piece, Mme de Bouillon requested that she come to her box. La Lecouvreur was extremely surprised and answered that she was not in proper attire and could not thus appear before her. The Duchesse sent a second time and to this summons Lecouvreur replied that though the Duchesse might pardon her appearing thus, the public would not, but that she would wait for the Duchesse as she was leaving in order to obey her orders.

Mme de Bouillon sent word that she should not fail to do so and, on leaving, she met the actress accordingly. She gave Lecouvreur all manner of caresses, praised her much on her acting and assured her of her infinite pleasure at having seen her so well execute the role she had performed.

The Duchesse was certainly intent on convincing Adrienne that she was not her enemy.

By the end of 1729 Adrienne's health was rapidly failing. Her suspicion of the Duchesse and Maurice's continued cruelty would be enough to shake any sensitive human being. But much more serious and painful for Adrienne was her dispute with Alexis Piron who had been her greatest author-admirer next to Voltaire. This author of *Métromanie* was reputed to be a man of letters, of impeccable wit, and great learning, and had been one of her intimate friends. Two years before, he had written her a lovely *Epître:*

> To Mademoiselle Lecouvreur who played the role of Angélique in my comedy "School for Fathers"
>
> A rival of Praxiteles
> And the Coustou of his century,

Carved a Venus, but so beautiful,
So beautiful that he went mad.

'Venus,' he cried out endlessly,
'Your glory moved my chisel!
Therefore serve my love now.
Animate this beautiful object!'

Venus heard his prayer:
And the stone began to breathe.
From that moment the sculptor
Loved no longer, he worshipped.

Soon he himself was loved;
And that which a thousand fools
Would envy as a supreme bounty—
He took all the credit for.

Shepherds, trace well upon the trees
What I have just told you:
Cupid can make even marble sigh:
That is the moral of the story.

And you, Goddess of the Stage,
To whom we offer incense each day,
You whom Thalia and Melpomene
Prefer to their own nurslings,

Queen of pleasant magic
And of sweet illusion,
Beautiful Lecouvreur, permit one more
Allusion to my Fable,

My Angélique is my statue,
And you have just brought her to life;
My Fable would be completely true,
If only you would deign to love me.[5]

After having promised her the principal role in his new
tragedy *Callisthène*, he withdrew it from her and con-
ferred it upon a newcomer to the Comédie, Mlle de Balin-

court. Attempting to disguise his bad will in well-turned phrases, he wrote Adrienne a letter: his excuse for having withdrawn the role from Adrienne had to do with personality and physical strength. He had conceived of a heroine more "severe"

> Mademoiselle,
> . . . Rest assured that there is no equal to my admiration for your talent except perhaps the respect that your noble mind inspires in me. I hope to prove both many more times before I die. But let us not reduce respect to impossible sacrifice. In this play I did not conceive of those seductive charms which are born of a tender sigh, a delicate glance, a silence, or a well-executed outcry, those triumphant *je ne sais quoi* in which subtle art and sweet nature are continually obliged to come to each other's aid. Rather did I conceive of austere, simple, and bare grace, in which all the art in the world could not replace what must not help nature. We must agree, Mademoiselle, that the charms of face, size, and body are proportionate to each other as they are predetermined.

As difficult as the letter must have been for Piron to write, he must have been quite proud of it. But his ego, vanity, and lack of tact prevented him from seeing that he would gravely wound its recipient.

> . . . The most engaging Venus is powerless when one expects the superb Pallas; and I believe that this role [Léonide] calls for more shield than girdle. The choice I have made was in my mind when I wrote the first words. It was upheld as I

progressed with the play and became more and
more confirmed as I finished it. You then had, as
you will always have on all other occasions,
absolute power over me. That comes from too far
beyond to mention it further. To dispute it would
honor me as it would afflict me. I will not always
conceive of Amazons as my heroines, and it will
not be long before I will call on the aid of your
talent to again lend success to my works. Then
you will prove to me that you are the generous
friend who will scold me for my shame. As for
me, I only seek in all and everywhere to prove to
you that no one has my greater respect and
attachment than you, Mademoiselle.

Your very humble and obedient servant,
Piron

January 9, 1730.

Adrienne replied quickly and to the point:

January 10, 1730.

Never has one used such art and such eloquence
to tell someone: "My success is impossible in
your hands." First, Monsieur, you had promised
me your role for some time; for I judge the
promise to have been all you meant it to be before
and since the reading of the first acts of your
play it pleased you to make in my home. The
confidence your simple manner inspired, the
friendship you displayed, and perhaps my own
vanity did not allow me to think for one moment
that there was any doubt in your choice. That is
why I demanded no further binding confirmation!
Besides, had I given you any reason to believe I
might refuse the role, you would have signed in
your own blood, and whatever I say here, rest
assured that I have no intention of making you

change your mind. I know the extent of your
zeal in supporting your opinions, as well as the
danger and disgust of constraining a man of wit
and imagination. I am also convinced that in all
things, I am worth nothing unless I am desired;
but I must justify myself for having dared to say
in open assembly of colleagues that I was to play
your role. I repeat, Monsieur, you did promise it
to me, just as you had promised the role of
Callisthène to our friend Sarazin.

Adrienne evidently believed her enemies in the troupe
influenced Piron to make his decision:

You have sacrificed both of us, not for the talents
of Mlle de Balincourt—although I admit she has
talent—but to your fear of Monsieur Quinault,
and where that is concerned, I strongly doubt
that you have the upper hand.

Piron was on very intimate terms with Mlle Quinault.
Mlle de Balincourt, a cousin of the Quinaults, had made
her debut in 1727:

Monsieur Quinault has more experience than
Monsieur Sarazin, but Sarazin has a newer and
surer feeling for success. The applause he received
and merited in his latest roles are a very real
proof. As for me, I find that you do me great
injustice in giving me praise I do not merit: I am
much further from resembling Venus than that
Pallas whom you measure with a rod; you forget
that, in the time of Mlles Desmares and Duclos, I
have played Roxanne, Athalie, Phèdre, Elisabeth,
Pauline and Cornélie, and the public did not seem
to complain of my weakness or my courage, and

I believe that soul is more necessary than size. I
have no quarrel over the charms or talent of the
one you prefer to me, but I do not think her
strength so superior to mine. You already have
the example of the Medea that she never played
more than twice a week without complaining
that she had spit blood, and the entire troupe will
tell you that she never plays without complaining
of fever or some other disposition. She does have
a love for the profession which I sincerely respect,
but which I think I have pushed much further
than she. Finally, the role of Léonide does not
call for a madwoman; those austere, simple, and
bare charms you desire will not be found any
more in her than in me, and for this I refer you to
those who see further than you do. For if it were
a question of an opposite comparison, and you
had told me that Mlle Dufresne or another ap-
proached a thousand times more closely those
graces you attribute to Venus and that girdle you
believe will crush me, I would say you are right
and even flatter myself for having warned you.
But I am much closer to the shield, since shield
and girdle there are. In a word, my soul is as
male and as sensitive to virtue as any you will
ever find. This is what made me admire your play
and what pleased me about [Léonide's] role. And
this is what makes me forgive you for an affront
that no other woman would ever forget. I say
"affront" because I said in open assembly that you
had promised it to me, and because after a career
made possible through the acclaim I still receive
from the public, through the friendship I have
shown you, and the sincere praise I have given
you, it is inconceivable that you would throw
yourself to another, and still more unreasonable
that you are giving your Callisthène to someone

171

other than your friend Sarazin. But fear of the
devil often makes more converts than the love of
God. This is what will console us.

Your very humble and obedient servant,
Lecouvreur.

On the very same day Adrienne wrote to a friend,
enclosing her correspondence with Piron, and it is difficult to decide whether her "consolation" was not one of
sour grapes. She was, after all, human:

I have lost the pleasure of playing a role which
pleased me, which I had accepted even before it
had been written, by a man whom I believed my
friend. But I have also lost the fear of making an
author unhappy or of displeasing the public, as
well as fatigue [of rehearsals] and the envy of
others. But I have gained, aside from rest, the
time to devote myself to the good company which
does me the honor to put up with me. This will
cost you more than one dinner.

After this incident Adrienne remained absent from the
theatre for three weeks, returning on February 4 to play
Electre before the Duc de Lorraine. On March 11, 1730,
nine days before her death, she wrote to her old friend,
the Marquis de la Chalotais who had become Avocat-
Général at Rennes and who had taken to sending her a
gift each year at Lent. Its beginning is worthy of the best
epistolary literature of the period:

I have received, Monsieur, the tribute which your
friendship causes you to send me each year at
Lent. I am annoyed that Lent comes but once a

year, because only in that season do you honor
me with some word of you. I am very flattered
that your emotion subsists in spite of the length
of time we have not seen each other and the slight
hope we have of ever doing so.

This was followed by reminiscences of times long since
past:

There you are honored with a mission which will
keep you more than ever in your beloved Brittany,
and unless I go there, I will never see my little
abbé. Perhaps it is not proper to speak this way
to a man who has become so solemn through the
sacrament and the magistrature. I therefore very
humbly ask, Monsieur, forgiveness from you,
from your wife, and from your new position. The
only assurance I can give you is that my little
abbé, full of wit, charm, and wisdom, was no
less respectable to me than was Monsieur le
Marquis de la Chalotais, father of a family and
avocat-général of the Parlement of Brittany.
These titles, far from imposing upon me, give me
license, it seems, to speak to you more innocently
and with more confidence of the feelings that an
extreme youth and a complete liberty ought to
have tempered. When ten or twelve years of
friendship combine with that special attachment
that resists distance and hurts no one, this gives
one liberty to speak without restraint. I assure
you, then, that my love equals my respect for
you and pray for your happiness and for your
family's. I beg you to remember me, and even
better than before.

On March 15, Mademoiselle Aïssé and her friend
Madame de Parabère, saw her for the last time in the part

173

of Jocaste in Voltaire's *Oedipe* and in Champmeslé's *Le Florentin:*

> Some time later, La Lecouvreur took ill in the middle of a play that could not be completed. When this was announced to the audience, the entire *parterre* demanded news of the actress. Since that day she wasted away and became horribly thin. Finally, her last performance was in the role of Jocaste in Voltaire's *Oedipe*, a very taxing role. Before the performance she had so strong an attack of dysentery that during the play she had to go to her dressing room twenty times where she vomited pure blood. The prostration and weakness of her condition were a pitiful sight to see; and, although I was unaware of her discomfort, I did remark two or three times to Mme de Parabère that her appearance was about to make me cry. Between the two plays we were told of her illness. We were surprised to see her reappear in the second play, the *Florentin*, in which she played a very long and difficult role which was carried out beautifully and which even she herself seemed to enjoy. We were all very grateful to her for having continued so that it could not be said, as once before, that she had been poisoned. The poor creature went home and four days later, at one in the afternoon, she died, just when she was thought to be out of danger.

Aïssé was mistaken concerning the date; Adrienne died five days after this performance.

Chapter Nine

THE DEMISE OF A
Great Actress

DRIENNE WAS STRICKEN on Wednesday, March 15, 1730. In her final moments a vicar was summoned from Saint-Sulpice. The church sent Languet de Gergy, known to be one of the more stubborn and bigoted priests in a time when there was no dearth of this type of cleric. It would appear that he exhorted Adrienne to make "an act of repentance of the scandals of her profession" and to sign the usual renuniciation of the theatre which the Church demanded before according the final sacraments. Adrienne is said to have refused. Tired by the priest's urging and horrified at the thought of her approaching death, she is supposed to have rebelled against God and destiny by holding out her hands towards a bust of Maurice and crying out: "There are my universe, my hope, and my gods!" Since we know that Maurice himself was at her bedside during her final hours, this occurrence seems unlikely.

She expired on Monday, March 20, between one and three in the afternoon. Besides Maurice de Saxe, Voltaire and the surgeon Faget were at her bedside. Her chambermaid reported: "When she died Messieurs de Saxe, Voltaire, and Faget the surgeon, were present, and they

175

departed immediately thereafter. D'Argental was notified of the death and he came at once." Not wanting to see the corpse, he went instead to a room on the third floor and instructed a servant to bring him the strongbox containing Adrienne's last will and testament. He thus began his duties as executor, Adrienne having named him *légataire universel* the previous April 7. By means of the will, a trust fund was created by which Adrienne assured her two daughters title to her fortune, but left very little to her sister, Marie-Marguerite. To her she bequeathed the amount of 560 *livres* a year for life, plus a lump sum payment of 4,000 *livres*.

This led to an attempt at character assassination by Marie-Marguerite, and her new husband. In their complaint which sought to inform the police of embezzlement and concealment of papers and documents at the moment of Adrienne's death, they used statements by servants which sought to prove that d'Argental "had much influence over her mind, was her principal advisor, conducted all her affairs, acted as though he were master of the house, and one referred to him simply as 'Monsieur' without adding his name." Thus it would appear that d'Argental had all the responsibilities of "Maître de la maison" without any of the advantages—for as we know, the true "monsieur" was not he.

There now arose the question of Adrienne's burial. To begin with, several of her neighbors had been previously incited against her by Marie-Marguerite, who had accused Adrienne of sequestering her in a small room, where she was fed only bread and water. These people now insisted on entering Adrienne's home to view the body and offer holy water. They laid seige to the doorway and were prevented from entering only with great difficulty. The servants, for their part, stole everything they could lay hands on. A valuable watch thought to have been brought from England by d'Argental disappeared from her bedroom and was never found.

On the morning of March 21, at the request of Adrienne's friends, an autopsy was performed. This resulted in a conclusion of death by natural causes. All that now remained was to arrange for burial.

Considering Adrienne's rumored refusal to repent, there was never a question of a religious service. Priests had the right to exclude from the churches the remains of those who had died unrepentant. Unfortunately, ecclesiastic authority also extended to cemeteries, thereby closing places of burial to the condemned.

Police lieutenant Hérault, acting on the order of Interior Minister Maurepas, was to see that the body was disposed of during the night of March 21, in order to avoid scandal. Maurepas had consulted with Cardinal de Fleury, who had no wish to intercede with the Archbishop of Paris and the priests of Saint-Sulpice: "If they persist in their refusal of a burial place, as they apparently do," wrote the Cardinal to Maurepas, "she will have to be removed by night and buried with the least scandal possible."

The lieutenant acted quickly. At midnight he sent a police officer named Laubinière who, with the help of two porters, placed the body on the bank of the Seine, near the rue de Bourgogne. After digging a hole, they laid in it a bed of quicklime on which they dropped the body. After sprinkling more quicklime over it, they filled in the earth and left.

The emotion of the populace turned into disbelief when news spread of the treatment of Adrienne's remains. But there were few, if any, who were bold enough to criticize openly an official act of authority. Thus the indignation of Adrienne's friends and admirers, as real as it was, had to remain discreet.

The following day, March 22, the Comédie-Française sat in extraordinary assembly. Voltaire was present and, so the story goes, exhorted the actors to declare "that they would refrain from exercising their profession until the King's players were treated like other citizens who do not have the honor to belong to the household of His Majesty." The actors are said to have agreed to this, but there is no record of any such action on their part. At their annual Holy Week recess, Grandval pronounced the traditional "compliment" which for this session had been written by Voltaire:

> I feel, gentlemen, that your sorrow recalls this inimitable actress, who had almost invented the art of speaking to the heart and of replacing pomp and declamation with sentiment and truth.

> Mlle Lecouvreur—permit us the consolation of naming her—in all her portrayals, brought out all the delicacy, all the soul, all the propriety you wished for; she was worthy of speaking before you, gentlemen; among those who do me the honor of hearing me here, there are several who honored her with their friendship; they know she was the ornament of society as well as the theatre, and those who knew her only as an actress can well judge, from the degree of perfection she had obtained, that not only did she

have great intelligence, but she knew the art of making her mind endeared.

You are all too right, gentlemen, in not considering this tribute of praise a duty: I even dare say that in mourning her, I am your spokesman.

Bouret did not budge from his original story during his first two interrogations, which took place in Saint-Lazare prison. Once transferred to the Bastille, however, on May 9, 1730, two months after Adrienne's death, his replies at the third interrogation showed many discrepancies and contradictions. It is here that he spoke for the first time of the actress Duclos, stating that he had met her on two or three occasions. In the same deposition he admitted having dined at her house with the actor Pierre-Jacques Duchemin, Mademoiselle Duclos' very young husband.

Bouret told of having first met Duchemin during the Pentecost season of 1729 in the *parterre* of the Comédie-Française, Bouret having complimented him on his previous night's performance. They met several days later at the Café Procope and became close friends. One month before his arrest, Bouret was still seeing Duchemin and dining at his house. Thus, about three weeks before his meeting with Adrienne, Bouret dined with Duchemin and Duclos. Bouret said that he did not speak of the poisoning scheme with Duchemin and his wife, feeling that he did not know them well enough and knowing also that "la Duclos was the sworn enemy of la Lecouvreur." At these dinners, there was one other guest, a woman named Rameau.

At this juncture it is necessary to relate some background material about Mlle Duclos whom we already know to have been the sworn enemy of Adrienne. Her marriage with Duchemin took place in 1725, when the bride was 55 and the groom 17 years of age. The marriage became a public joke at once. It was never a happy one and, from 1727 on, according to Duclos' complaints against her husband, he beat her. She demanded an annulment. Curiously, it was Duchemin who finally left Duclos in February 1730, lodging a complaint against the above-mentioned Rameau, her *confidente*.

Rameau's place in Duclos' life takes on interesting possibilities only when one recalls the circumstances involving Mlle Duclos and the "Chevalier de Morsan" which occurred in the six years preceding her marriage to Duchemin.

Her marriage to Duchemin at the height of the scandal did nothing to put an end to the rumors. Duchemin, barely seventeen, was hardly a man, and poor Duclos continued to be the object of the public's merriment. May we thus assume that the *confidente* Rameau was more than that to Duclos? Duchemin, in his complaint against Rameau, spoke of her hold over his wife and blamed her for their separation.

In the light of the Abbé's own statements, it is not difficult to imagine him in these surroundings. It would appear that he was not unfamiliar with practices considered questionable by the larger part of society. What were his reasons after all, for going from one private box to another at the theatre? Was he actually on familiar terms with the well-to-do occupants of these accommodations? He certainly would not find the same element of society standing in the *parterre*. Yet this is where he met Duchemin. How was it possible that this physically-deformed monk was able to strike up a close relationship with a well-known young actor? Why was it so easy for him to form close relationships with young men of varying stations?

We cannot totally ignore the possibility that Bouret invented the whole bizarre tale in order to obtain access to Adrienne—although his means for doing so were as uncertain as they were dangerous. On the other hand, the Duchesse's scheme, as reported by Bouret, is certainly not impossible, considering the character of the woman in question, and the fact that she was passionately in love. It is even possible that Bouret lied and persisted in his lie once the story became public. What speaks in his favor, however, is not that he persisted in his story, but that his insistence on its truth was to last long after Adrienne's death, long after any visible possibility of reward, and in spite of the tempting promise of liberty in exchange for a retraction.

The judicial inquest left much to be desired. Carried on with scandalous carelessness, its sole objective seems to have been to obtain from Bouret a retraction. Once this was accomplished, Bouret was held nine more months, possibly to guarantee his silence.

If the Duchesse was innocent, it surely would have been to her interest to make certain that the case was prosecuted according to the most correct procedures of justice. Whatever her reasons for not seeing to this, we at least may assume that fear of scandal did not enter into her reasoning. The scandal had already taken place. Nor could she have feared a renewal of the scandal, since she continued to remain suspect, as indeed she still remains.

The Abbé Aunillon must have wondered about this himself. Hard-pressed to explain the lack of action on the part of the Duchesse, he gave this as the reason:

> Bouret would have been guilty and worthy of the supreme punishment for such avowed slander, if he himself could be suspected of bad faith. But several circumstances in his interrogations prove only too well that another person of consideration, *whom it is useless to name* [italics added], had set the machine in motion, not in order to poison La Lecouvreur, but to ruin the reputation of the unfortunate Duchesse. To the detriment of the Duchesse, extremely strong considerations stopped all those who had as much interest as she in a public justification; but this could be done only at the expense of denouncing before the public and the courts she who in fact was guilty of such a vilification. The Duchesse was thus obliged to be content with the statement of the painter that he had never seen, painted, or known her, once he was confronted with everyone concerned with the affair; and her only consolation was the witness of her own conscience and the conviction of her friends and family.

Thanks to the Archives of the Bastille, preserved by the Bibliothèque de l'Arsenal in Paris, we have the detailed record of the interrogations Aunillon refers to, containing the depositions obtained from Bouret. Curiously enough, on close examination, it would appear that the part of Aunillon's explanation having to do with a scheme by a person other than the Duchesse is possible and even probable. Given the sexual proclivities of the Mesdemoiselles of the Comédie-Française, and with specific reference both to Duclos' special tastes and to Adrienne's relationship with Mademoiselle, this other "person of consideration" might very well have been a jealous and rejected lover. We are reluctant to dismiss this possibility.

Among documents published much later, we find one relating to a complaint by Adrienne against a former lackey who had returned to her house and proceeded to throw stones through her windows. He was arrested on the spot and imprisoned. We do not know how long he remained there or whether he was ever released. On another occasion, her servant and *confident* La Roche had been imprisoned for an offense committed against one of Adrienne's guests who complained that he had stolen her wrap. La Roche, too, was present at Adrienne's death, having just previously been released from prison with her help. When word of Adrienne's death had spread, La Roche did all in his power to bar outsiders from entering the house, insisting that she had not died. Lastly, the name of La Roche often appears in the already mentioned complaint against d'Argental lodged by Adrienne's sister. Marie-Marguerite accused La Roche of threatening her with bodily harm if she persisted in her claim to the inheritance.

Is it not curious that the Abbé Bouret had direct contacts in these diverse directions, with the possible exception of the last? He dined at the home of Adrienne's enemy, having been invited by her young husband whose acquaintance he had made in the *parterre* of the Comédie-Française. He formed a friendship with a handsome young page in the employ of the Duchesse de Bouillon, begin-

183

ning his portrait in miniature on the morning following their meeting, and regularly visiting the Saint-Germain fair accompanied by him. It is entirely possible that this page was related in some way either to Adrienne's former lackey or to La Roche, both of whom were imprisoned for reasons which are still not too clear. That the Duchesse employed the page does not prove that the Abbé actually met her. Although his first-hand description of her apartment is quite believable, the page could very well have allowed Bouret to see it in the Duchesse's absence. As handsome as he was, the page could very likely have been an object of the Duchesse's all-inclusive taste, thereby causing him to bear her a grudge. Biographers and historians have generally ignored the important fact that in 1729 the Duchesse was but 22 years old. The page, for his part, aware of his special power over Bouret, could have used him in a two-fold scheme to ruin the Duchesse's reputation and/or to avenge the bad treatment of friends or relatives unjustly sent to prison. Thus, it is possible that the Abbé kept to his original accusation of the Duchesse either to prove his love and loyalty to the page, or to keep the true plot, with all its implications, from ever being known.

Whichever quarter was first to act upon its hate for Adrienne, it is probable that this action took the form of an attempt at poisoning. If the attempt was the Duchesse's there is nothing to indicate that, having failed with the Abbé, she renewed her attempt during the evening at the theatre described in Aïssé's letter. Under suspicion for several months, tormented by overt rumors, despised for the continued imprisonment of Bouret, no matter how decided the Duchesse may have been to rid herself of Adrienne, simple prudence would have dictated that she wait.

What is much more certain is that Adrienne's health had been very unsteady and that she was absent from the theatre for long periods of time. There are numerous allusions in her correspondence to her poor state of health. As early as 1720 she wrote: "I have not had twelve hours of health since I last saw you." She spoke of an "unbearable fatigue" which continually plagued her: "I am not at all well. My health is driving me to despair, and I cannot control the sadness it inflicts upon me. I find it more difficult to make the best of an eternal decline than a live and well-stated illness." Subject to chronic intestinal disorders, Adrienne had almost died of dysentery in 1725 and 1726. Following a series of huge doses of a potent remedy, she finally did succumb to acute dysentery. Aïssé's mention that convulsions never occur in cases of this sort is, of course, not correct. Muscular spasms do often accompany violent intestinal disorders.

All possibilities thus considered, we must conclude in favor of a natural death. There is nothing to confirm the theory of a successful second attempt at poisoning. There was very probably an unsuccessful first attempt, but it is more than likely that the perpetrator was not the Duchesse. We have shown that there is a possibility that the Abbé Aunillon was correct when he stated that other persons of high rank had attempted to damage the Duchesse's reputation. However, the suggestions of Duclos/Duchemin/Rameau on one hand, and the page/lackey/La Roche group on the other, each having direct contact with Bouret, seem much more tenable.

Chapter Ten

THE BIRTH OF
The Legend

A S WE HAVE seen, Adrienne died during Bouret's judicial inquest, and Bouret was transferred to the Bastille, where he persisted in his original accusation of the Duchesse. A letter to Hérault from Père de Couvrigny, Jesuit confessor of the Bastille, confirmed the attitude of Bouret: "He appears firm in insisting that he does no calumny against others, but neither could he do any against himself; the affair is quite terrible and serious."

This note was dated May 18, 1730. The Abbé was still in prison on July 8, 1730, his arrest having taken place on July 29, 1729. For his part, Bouret also wrote to Hérault:

> To deviate from my story, death with all its horrors could appear before my eyes, I would embrace it rather than slander myself; what interest, for what reason would I have thrown myself into the labyrinth I now find myself?

On August 24, 1730, the Abbé completely changed his mind. Hérault, whatever methods he may have used, succeeded in obtaining the following retraction:

> As you have done me the honor of ordering me to tell the truth concerning Madame la Duchesse

187

de Bouillon, I surrender to your orders. Here it is. My desire to know La Lecouvreur caused me to think up a means for gaining entry to her house . . . I declare that Madame la Duchesse is innocent of everything I have said. . . . Forgive a miserable being whose only crime is a muddled brain and a great deal of imprudence.

After the retraction, the unfortunate Abbé had to wait more than nine months before being released. Freed on June 3, 1731, after nearly two years of confinement, there is no further trace of him.

The *Mercure de France*, in its long obituary calling for public mourning, did not dare to print one word concerning Adrienne's burial. It would appear that only the poets of the time were able to express feelings which could be made public nowhere else. One of the first to compose a poetic epitaph was Adrienne's old friend, the Marquis de Rochemore:

> ⚜ *Cy gît l'actrice inimitable*
> *De qui l'esprit et les talents,*
> *Les Grâces et les sentiments*
> *La rendaient partout adorable;*
> *Et qui n'a pas moins mérité*
> *Le droit à l'immortalité*
> *Qu'aucune Héroïne ou Déesse,*
> *Qu'avec tant de délicatesse*
> *Elle a souvent représenté.*
>
> *L'opinion était si forte*
> *Qu'elle devait toujours durer,*
> *Qu'après même qu'elle fut morte*
> *On refusa de l'enterrer.*

> ⚜ Here lies the inimitable actress
> Whose mind and talent,

THE BIRTH OF THE LEGEND

> Grace and sentiments
> Made her everywhere loved;
> And who did no less merit
> The right to immortality
> Than any heroine or goddess
> That, with so much delicacy,
> She often portrayed.
>
> There was so strong an opinion
> That she would last forever,
> That even after she had died,
> They refused to bury her.

Another, René de Bonneval, was deeply critical of the Church's refusal to grant a place of burial:

> What contrast strikes our eyes!
> Melpomene here in grief
> Raises, with the help of the Gods,
> A magnificent Mausoleum;
> Here superstition,
> Fearing even the dust,
> Makes a point of religion
> To cover with it a gentle soul.
> Illustrious spirit, be consoled,
> In all places the earth is equal.
> When fatal Parque
> Makes us succumb to her sad law,
> What does it matter where our remains
> Must repose, to await
> That time when all prejudice
> Will forever be forsworn.
> Places are no longer profane
> Once they are the abode of illustrious spirits.
> Your tomb will be respected,
> And if it is not often frequented
> By reciters of Our Fathers,
> It will doubtlessly be visited by others

189

Whose more natural homage
Must render your name immortal.
In place of tiresome matins,
The Graces, wearing mourning,
Will sing divine hymns
Each morning over your grave.
Sophocles, Corneille, Racine
Will endlessly spread flowers,
While Jocasta and Pauline
Will shed a torrent of tears.
Finally, for your apotheosis,
They will compose an Ode in prose:
This masterpiece, from the pen of a *bel-esprit*
Will be worth at least as much as a Requiem.
Fi, then, on this injustice
Which refuses your body
That which Pelletier des Forts obtained
Through an even more astounding whim.*
This impious and criminal spirit,
To the shame of the French name,
With the support of our laws,
Will one day shine inside a chapel.
Thus, through some bizarre fate,
This harsh and barbarous Minister,
Must repose in splendor,
While, with disgrace,
To the emulator of Cornélie
They refuse the same honor.[6]

And this by an anonymous poet:

Why then be informed where La Lecouvreur lies?
For her glory and honor,
What does it matter where her ashes repose?
You who knew her, give her altars

* Pelletier des Forts, *contrôleur-général*, was dismissed in disgrace
from the Ministry.

And give her the incense due to the immortals;
    But leaving off her apotheosis,
Let us rather say that instead of having left us,
La Lecouvreur has only changed her place of
    abode;
That she who made the honor of our stage,
She of whom all Paris, her long-time admirer,
    Finally became idolatrous,
She for whom Jocasta, to the delight of the
    audience,
Could excite pity and terror,
She finally, who with her supreme talent,
Depicted Phaedra's love, hate, and madness,
    Was Melpomene herself
    Under the name of La Lecouvreur.
    Why bury her then?
Are the tombs of the gods among us mortals?
    They made the earth for us,
It is for them that they made the heavens.

Alexis Piron himself, forgetting their quarrel, offered this homage to Adrienne:

    ⚜ *L'Enfer, abondant en supplices,*
       Est doublement notre bourreau:
       En nous enlevant nos délices,
       En nous laissant notre fléau.

       O comble affreux, mais peu nouveau,
       De ces horreurs dont il s'honore!
       La Lecouvreur est au tombeau
       Et son médecin vit encore!

    ⚜ Hades, abundant in torture,
       Is doubly our executioner:
       By taking away our delights,
       By leaving behind the scourge.

O height of horrors, but hardly new,
With which it honors itself!
La Lecouvreur is in the tomb . . .
And her doctor is still alive!

Seven months after Adrienne's death, a renowned English actress, Anne Oldfield, died in London. After a state funeral, she was buried in Westminster Abbey. Voltaire could no longer hold back his amazement at the contrast of similar affairs in two different countries. He wrote the famous elegy that gave rise to the series of persecutions which caused him to flee Paris.

In a letter to Thierot in which he first enclosed the poem, he wrote: "I cannot hold on to these verses which came to me out of indignation, affection, and pity, and in which, by mourning for Mlle Lecouvreur, I join my feeble voice to all the voices of England in order to make a little understood the difference between their liberty and our slavery, their wise boldness and our mad superstition, the encouragement that the arts receive in London and the shameful oppression under which they languish in Paris."

On the Death of Mlle Lecouvreur, famous actress

What see I? what object! what! these charming
    lips,
What! these eyes, fountains of eloquent flame,
Are sustaining the ghastly horrors of death!
Muses, Graces, Cupids, whose image she was,
O my gods and hers, come to the aid of your
    masterpiece!
What see I? it is done with, I kiss you, and you
    die!
You die; the terrible news has already spread!
My mortal sorrow has moved all hearts.

192

Everywhere I hear the bewildered fine-arts
Cry out in tears: "Melpomene is no more!"
What will you say, future race,
When you learn of the slurring insult
That cruel priests perform upon these grieved
    arts?
        An object worthy of altars
        Is deprived of a tomb!
And into a profane field the immortal remains
Of this so cherished body are thrown at random!
No, this bank henceforth is no longer profane,
It contains your ashes; and this sad tomb,
Honored by our song, consecrated by your spirit,
        Is for us a new temple!
Here is my Saint-Denis; yes, it is here I adore
Your talent, your mind, your graces, your
    charms:
I loved them alive, I still burn incense to them
        Despite death's horrors,
        Despite the error and the thankless ones
Whose infamy alone is dishonored in this tomb.
Ah! will I always see my weak nation,
Uncertain in vows, sully that which it adores,
Our manners always contradict our laws,
And the fickle Frenchman asleep under the
    domain
        Of superstition?
        What! is it then only in England
        That mortals dare think?
O rival to Athens, O London! happy land!
As you did with tyrants, you also chased away
Shameful prejudices which brought you war.
There they know how to say all and reward all;
No art is scorned, each success has its glory;
The victor of Tallard, Victory's son,
Sublime Dryden, and Wise Addison,
And charming Ophils, and the immortal Newton,
        Share in the Temple of Memory:

And in London Lecouvreur would have had a
    tomb
Amidst the great minds, the kings, and the heroes.
In London, whoever has talent is a great man.
    Abundance and freedom
Have, after two thousand years, brought back in
    you
      The spirit of Greece and Rome.
Is the neglected leaf of Apollo's laurels
Trampled then in our sterile fields?
Gods! why is my country no longer the land
      Of both glory and talent? [7]

Voltaire was never to forget this insult to his dear friend and to a profession he loved. Allusions to Adrienne's death and burial appear throughout his works and correspondence.

When Candide goes to the theatre with Pangloss and Martin and asks a stranger how great actresses are treated in France, he is told that they are "adored when they are beautiful and thrown into the gutter when they are dead." When Candide expresses his amazement, Martin answers: "I was in Paris when Mademoiselle Monime passed, as they say, from this life to the next; she was refused what those people call the honors of the sepulchre, that is, to rot with all the beggars of the quarter in a dirty cemetery; alone of her profession, she was buried at the corner of the rue de Bourgogne; which must have been very painful to her since she had a very noble mind."

As to the exact location of Adrienne's place of burial, the earliest indication comes from the second edition of *Zaïre* whose editor called the area *La Grenouillière*, which would place it at the southeast corner of the rue de Grenelle and the rue de Bourgogne. When the century and d'Argental were both 86 years old, he went to this spot where he composed the following *huitain* and had it engraved on a marble plaque which he himself set into a neighboring wall. The old wall now forms the inside of the courtyard at number 115, rue de Grenelle:

⚜ *Ici l'on rend hommage à l'actrice admirable,*
Par l'esprit, par le coeur également aimable.
Un talent vrai, sublime en sa simplicité,
L'appelait, par nos voeux, à l'immortalité;
Mais le sensible effort d'une amitié sincère
Put à peine obtenir ce petit coin de terre;
Et le juste tribut du plus pur sentiment
Honore enfin ce lieu méconnu si longtemps.

⚜ We render here homage to the admirable
    actress
Who for mind and heart was equally adored,
A true talent, sublime in its simplicity,
Called her, through our wishes, to immor-
    tality;
But the sensitive effort of a sincere friendship
Could obtain nothing more than this small
    piece of earth;
And the just tribute of purest sentiment
Finally honors this place so long lost.

At the end of the century, more than 60 years after Adrienne's death, and with the new freedom that came with the Revolution, the Comédie-Française addressed the following letter to the Minister of the Interior of the Republic, citizen Benezech:

Paris, 8 Floreal, year V.

We address ourselves to you with confidence to obtain an act of equity invoked by the fine arts, whose friend and protector you are.

195

Shameful prejudice, fanaticism, and superstition refused in former times the honors of sepulchre to the renowned Adrienne Lecouvreur. This touching actress, the first to bring to the tragic stage the language of nature, the outcry of the soul, and the expression of truth, received on her death, as a reward for her talents, an outrage which demands reparation in the name of her spirit today in the century of philosophy, by a regenerate people who no longer know any authority foreign to her glory.

When our proud enemies placed amidst the tombs of their kings in Westminster, the tombs of Mistress Oldfield and Garrick, our ancestors ignominiously relegated the remains of Adrienne Lecouvreur outside the sepulchre accorded to what was called "the faithful," on the banks of the Seine, in unmarked ground, where nothing spelled out or recalled to the memory of men the precious deposit confined there!

We request, citizen Minister, that you authorize us to search out what might remain of a famous woman, to transport her mortal remains to the place designated by law as a final shelter for French citizens, and to cover the place occupied by these too-long-vilified remains, with a stone which will at least tell any friend of the Arts that there reposes an artist who was the delight of her century, and who was shamelessly abandoned by her century to barbarous laws written out of fanaticism and consecrated out of vile prejudice.

The Artists of the Theatre
of the Republic.

Citizen Benezech, however, soon fell from power, and things remained where they were. But the legacy of

Adrienne Lecouvreur was to continue throughout the nineteenth century as indeed it continues in our own.

It seems appropriate that Adrienne has not been forgotten by the municipal government of present-day Paris. One need only stand on the Champs-de-Mars facing the Ecole Militaire and then stroll toward the left. He will discover that the final path leading from the Eiffel Tower to the Ecole Militaire is called the Allée Adrienne Lecouvreur. If one is at a loss to understand why the authorities chose to honor Adrienne in these surroundings, by no means a short distance from the Comédie-Française, one need only continue walking toward the Ecole Militaire, entering through the main gate, walking straight ahead, and emerging on its opposite side. Any puzzlement will be instantly and delightfully solved with the discovery that one is standing at the foot of the Avenue de Saxe. In other words, the Allée and the Avenue would be one if they were not cut in two by the Ecole Militaire, the building over which Maurice doubtlessly presided when he later became Maréchal de France. To our knowledge, no "dictionnaire topographique" of the City of Paris has taken notice of this happy coincidence.

NOTES

Notes

---

[1] *The Portraits of Adrienne Lecouvreur*

The relative merit of the Drevet and Schmidt engravings was the subject of a public dispute between two eminent critics at the end of the last century: Georges Monval, Archivist of the Comédie-Française, and Gustave Larroumet, Director of the Ecole des Beaux-Arts.

Wishing to explain his reasons for having chosen the Schmidt engraving for his frontispiece (*Lettres d'Adrienne Lecouvreur*, 1892), Monval recognized the difficulty of ascertaining the authenticity of either portrait:

> Can one be sure, for example, of possessing today an authentic portrait of Molière? The absence of authentic documents permitted a certain critic of the grand comedy a short while ago to declare that Molière was ugly, and this hazarded affirmation has taken on a certain gravity since its author has since occupied the post of Director of the Ecole des Beaux-Arts.

The critic referred to by Monval was Gustave Larroumet whose publication on Adrienne's correspondence appeared shortly thereafter (*Adrienne Lecouvreur d'Après sa Correspondence*, 1892). This is his reply to Monval:

> Several actresses combine beauty with scenic qualities. Was Adrienne of that number? I hesitate

to examine the question with the use of contemporary witnesses for in an inquest of this type I have already run into the severity of Monsieur Georges Monval. It is well known that the knowledgable archivist is the high priest of the religion of Molière. Several years ago I wrote, concerning Molière, that, when one compares his portraits, one was obliged to say that he was ugly; but I hastened to add that "the interior flame of genius imparts to irregular features a beauty of a superior order." This oratorical precaution was not enough to avoid Monsieur Monval's onslaught.

Alluding to Monval's distress with a director of the Ecole des Beaux Arts who could have held such an opinion, Larroumet added:

> I did not know that the holder of this office had the privilege of distributing at will certificates of ugliness or beauty. This could be a powerful means of government which I point out to my successor. Be that as it may, and at the risk of finding myself once more in disagreement with Monsieur Monval, where Adrienne is concerned, I cannot avoid the question which, for Molière, brought on that sincerely felt accusation.

Larroumet did go on, however, to a discussion, point by point, of the comparative merits of the two portraits. Monval, who had referred to the Coypel/Drevet portrait as a "painting of fantasy and affectation; a study, banal figure, under which could also have been engraved the names of Madeleine repenting or of Sophie Arnould," was accused by Larroumet of lacking originality for having adopted the opinion of a third critic. He pointed out

202

that Régnier, five years earlier, had described the portrait in similar terms. Régnier had written that the portrait was of a "banal character, a study, as it is called at the School of Fine Arts." For his part, Larroumet praised the portrait, referring to Michelet who had called it "more than a work of art, a dream of pain, one of those encounters that one regrets with a unique person who will never return and from whom one is separated by the ravages of time."

In Monval's opinion there is not one portrait of Adrienne which is "original and faithful." Larroumet countered with his own description of the Drevet/Coypel portrait:

> "Those heavenly eyes, full of sublime tears which bring on others," to quote Michelet, the gesture of those arms holding the funeral urn, the shattering gentleness of that physiognomy, the silent accusation that the face flings against destiny, as many traits to make the portrait a unique work, the honor of the artist and the model. All this, I insist, is not resemblance; but, aside from the fact that nothing authorizes refusing the portrait the merit of being "original," for it was painted while Adrienne was alive, one could neither pretend that it is not "faithful" because we have nothing to compare it with.

Monval had preferred the Fontaine/Schmidt portrait because it depicted an Adrienne "truer, more human, alive, familiar, in which we find the woman rather than the actress; it is a Lecouvreur in *robe de chambre* such as she appeared amongst her friends." Larroumet was quick to point out that the Fontaine portrait bore a date after the death of Adrienne and he was not at all certain that Adrienne was indeed wearing a *robe de chambre:*

> The arrangement of Fontaine's painting with its well-coiffed hairdo, bare neck, very arranged silken dress, the "bouffant" mantle, denote, on the contrary, a showy portrait; in sum, it is a mediocre work with awkward pose, a summery outline for as much as one can judge from the transposition of the engraving which is itself a poor work.

For our part, we do have a preference for the dramatic Coypel/Drevet work; however, it must be added that when the two portraits are placed side by side, the physical resemblance is remarkable. We find the same high forehead, large deep eyes, slightly curved nose, delicate mouth, and rounded chin.

[2] Monval (*Lettres*, p. 22, n. 3) says that the house purchased by Adrienne, "*connue sous le nom d'Hôtel de Rannes (No. 21, actuel de la rue Visconti), avait été acquise en 1713 par Louis d'Argouges, Marquis de Rannes, Maréchal de camp. Racine y était mort en 1699.*" Henri Lyonnet confirmed this with certain reservations (*Les Comédiennes*, p. 13): "*A Paris, nous retrouvons Adrienne d'abord établie rue de Tournon, puis rue des Marais (rue Visconti actuelle, No. 21), dans une maison connue sous le nom de l'Hôtel de Rannes,* presque en face [our emphasis] *de celle où Racine était mort (maison disparue entre le 24 et l'angle de la rue Bonaparte).*" Lyonnet would thus appear to be saying that Adrienne did indeed live in the house which today bears the number 21 rue

Visconti, but that this could not be the house in which Racine had died. If this is true, then the commemorative plaque on Racine's death which still appears there is not correct. Monval seems to have drawn his information from a notation by Mlle Clairon: *"On me parla d'une petite maison, rue des Marais, du prix de 1200 livres. On me dit que Racine y avait demeuré, que c'était là qu'il était mort; qu'ensuite la touchante Lecouvreur l'avait occupée, ornée, et qu'elle y était morte aussi. . . . On me l'accorda,"* (*Mémoires* [Paris: Ponthieu, 1822], p. 19). Our own investigation led to a publication by Girault de Saint-Fargeau entitled *Les Quarante-huit quartiers de Paris* (Paris: Firmen, Didot, 1846), and another by Frédéric Lock, *Dictionnaire topographique et historique de l'ancien Paris* (Paris: Hachette, 1860). Both authors stated that the house in question, that is, the one in which Racine died, was number 19. Lock added that the house no longer existed at the time he was writing his book. Then, on a page of *errata*, Lock reversed himself, saying that the house was still standing and that it now was number 21. According to Paul Mesnard, who accompanied his edition of Racine's works (Paris: Hachette, 1865–73) with a volume of engravings which includes one by M. H. Clerget showing a view of the house in its then-present state, it would be the house which today bears the number 13. The Vicomte de Gruchy, in his *Documents inédits relatifs à Jean Racine* (Paris: Techener, 1892), p. 13, n. 1, adopted Mesnard's view that the house is number 13. Obviously there are contradictory findings concerning the house lived in by Racine. As for the house purchased by Adrienne, there are no opinions opposing the fact that it was the Hôtel de Rannes, but our investigation does lead to conflicting evidence. One of the documents published by Compardon in his *Comédiens du roi* (Paris: Champion, 1871), tells of a complaint lodged by Adrienne against a former *laquais* who had taken to throwing stones at the windows of her house. The police report tells of going to her house *"rue des Marais, et étant entré dans une maison* au milieu de la rue . . . ,"* [our emphasis]. If then, the Hôtel de Rannes was in the middle of the street, it is quite possible that it was, as Lyonnet stated, almost opposite Racine's house, but *on the same side of the street* as his. They could have faced each other across an *impasse* or *ruelle* which would have disappeared the moment either of the two houses was destroyed. It should also be pointed out that the French system of house numbering usually takes no notice of even and odd progressions, numbering all buildings on one side of a street consecutively.

[3] *Epître à Mademoiselle Lecouvreur*

> L'heureux talent dont vous charmez la France
> Avait en vous brillé dès votre enfance.
> Il fut dès lors dangereux de vous voir,
> Et vous plaisiez même sans le savoir.
> Sur le théâtre heureusement conduite,
> Parmi les voeux de cent coeurs empressés
> Vous récitiez, par la nature instruite:
> C'était beaucoup, ce n'était point assez.
> Il vous fallut encore un plus grand maître;
> Permettez-moi de faire ici connaître
> Quel est ce Dieu de qui l'art enchanteur
> Vous a donné votre gloire suprême,
> Le tendre Amour me l'a conté lui-meme.
> On me dira que l'Amour est menteur,
> Hélas! je sais qu'il faut qu'on s'en défie.

Qui mieux que moi connaît sa perfidie?
Qui souffre plus de sa déloyauté?
Je ne croirai cet enfant de ma vie.
Mais cette fois il a dit vérité,
Ce même Amour, Vénus et Melpomène
Loin de Paris faisaient voyage un jour.
Ces Dieux charmants vinrent dans un séjour
Où vos attraits éclataient sur la scène.
Chacun des trois avec étonnement
Vit cette grâce et simple et naturelle
Qui faisait lors votre unique ornement.
Mérite bien que sans retardement
Nous répandions tous nos trésors sur elle.
Ce qu'un Dieu veut se fait dans le moment.
Tout aussitôt la tragique Déesse
Vous inspira le goût, le sentiment,
Le pathétique et la délicatesse.
"Moi, dit Vénus, je lui fais un présent
Plus précieux, et c'est le don de plaire.
Elle accroîtra l'Empire de Cythère:
A son aspect tout coeur sera troublé,
Tous les esprits viendront lui rendre hommage."
—"Moi, dit l'Amour, je ferai davantage,
Je veux qu'elle aime!" A peine eut-il parlé
Que dans l'instant vous devîntes parfaite:
Sans aucuns soins, sans étude, sans fard,
Des Passions vous fûtes l'interprète.
O de l'Amour adorable sujette,
N'oubliez pas le secret de votre art.

Voltaire

4 *Portrait de M. de Fontenelle*

Les personnes ignorées font trop peu d'honneur
à celles dont elles parlent, pour oser mettre au
grand jour ce que je pense de M. de Fontenelle;
mais je ne puis me refuser en secret le plaisir de le
peindre ici tel qu'il me paraît.

Sa physionomie annonce d'abord son esprit; un air du monde, répandu dans toute sa personne, le rend aimable dans toutes ses actions.

Les agréments de l'esprit en excluent souvent les parties essentielles; unique en son genre, il rassemble tout ce qui fait aimer et respecter la probité. La droiture, l'équité composent son caractère. Une imagination vive, brillante, tours fins et délicats, expressions nouvelles et toujours heureuses, en font l'ornement. Le coeur pur, les procédés nets, la conduite uniforme, et par tout des principes, exigeant peu, justifiant tout, saisissant toujours le bon, abandonnant si fort le mauvais que l'on pourrait douter s'il l'a aperçu; difficile à acquérir, mais plus difficile à perdre; exact en amitié, scrupuleux en amour. L'honnête homme n'est négligé nulle part, propre aux commerces les plus délicats, quoique les délices des savants. Modeste dans ses discours, simple dans ses actions, la supériorité de son mérite se montre, mais il ne la fait jamais sentir.

De pareilles dispositions persuadent aisément le calme de son âme; aussi la possède-t-il si fort en paix, que la malignité de l'envie n'a point eu encore le pouvoir de l'ébranler.

Enfin, l'on pourrait dire de lui, ce qui a été déjà dit d'un illustre, qu'il fait honneur à l'homme, et que si ses vertus ne le rendent immortel, elles le rendent au moins très digne de l'être.

[5] *A Mademoiselle Lecouvreur qui jouait le rôle d'Angélique dans ma comédie de "l'Ecole des Pères"*

Un émule de Praxitèle
Et de son siècle le Coustou,

Fit une Vénus, mais si belle,
Si belle, qu'il en devint fou.

Venus, s'écriait-il sans cesse,
Ta gloire animait mon ciseau!
Sers donc maintenant ma tendresse!
Anime cet objet si beau!

Vénus entendit sa prière:
La pierre en effet respira.
De ce moment le statuaire
N'aima plus, il idolâtra.

Bientôt il fut aimé lui-même;
Et ce que mille extravagants
Envieraient comme un Bien suprême,
A coup sur il en eut les gants.

Bergers, gravez bien sur les arbres
Ce que je viens de vous narrer;
L'Amour peut attendrir les marbres:
C'est le sens qu'il en faut tirer.

Et vous, Déesse de la Scène,
Que tous les jours nous encensons,
Vous que Thalie et Melpomène
Préfèrent à leurs nourrissons,

Reine du prestige agréable
Et de la douce illusion,
Belle Lecouvreur, à ma Fable
Souffrez une autre allusion,

Mon Angélique est ma statue,
Et vous venez de l'animer;
Ma Fable est la vérité nue,
Pour peu que vous veuilliez m'aimer.

                                        Piron.

⁶ *A Mlle Lecouvreur*
Sur le refus qu'on a fait de l'enterrer (1730)

Quel contraste frappe nos yeux!
Melpomène ici désolée
Elève avec l'aveu des Dieux
Un magnifique Mausolée,
Ici la superstition,
Distinguant jusqu'à la poussière,
Fait un point de religion
D'en couvrir une âme légère.
Ombre illustre, console-toi,
En tous lieux la terre est égale.
Alors que la Parque fatale
Nous fait subir sa triste loi,
Peu nous importe où notre cendre
Doive reposer, pour attendre
Ce temps où tous les préjugés
Seront pour jamais abrogés.
Les lieux cessent d'être profanes
En contenant d'illustres mânes.
Ton tombeau sera respecté,
Et s'il n'est souvent fréquenté
Par les diseurs de patenôtres,
Sans doute il le sera par d'autres
Dont l'hommage plus naturel
Doit rendre ton nom immortel.
Au lieu d'ennuyeuses matines,
Les Grâces en habit de deuil
Chanteront des hymnes divines
Tous les matins sur ton cercueil.
Sophocle, Corneille, Racine
Sans cesse répandront des fleurs,
Tandis que Jocaste et Pauline
Verseront un torrent de pleurs.
Enfin pour ton apothéose

On doit te faire une Ode en prose:
Ce chef-d'oeuvre d'un bel esprit
Vaudra bien du moins un obit.
Méprise donc cette injustice
Qui fait refuser à ton corps
Ce que par un plus grand caprice
Obtiendra Pelletier des Forts,
Cette ombre impie et criminelle,
A la honte du nom françois,
Quelque jour dans une chapelle
Brillera sous l'appui des loix.
Ainsi par un destin bizarre
Ce Ministre dur et barbare
Doit reposer avec splendeur,
Tandis qu'avec ignominie
A l'émule de Cornélie
On refuse le même honneur.

René de Bonneval.

7 *La Mort de Mlle Lecouvreur, célèbre actrice*

Que vois-je? quel objet! quoi! ces lèvres
    charmantes,
Quoi! ces yeux d'où partaient ces flammes
    éloquentes,
Eprouvent du trépas les livides horreurs!
Muses, Grâces, Amours, dont elle fut l'image,
O mes dieux et les siens, secourez votre ouvrage!
Que vois-je? c'en est fait, je t'embrasse, et tu
    meurs!
Tu meurs; on sait déjà cette affreuse nouvelle;
Tous les coeurs sont émus de ma douleur mortelle.
J'entends de tous côtés les beaux-arts éperdus
S'écrier en pleurant: "Melpomène n'est plus!"
    Que direz-vous, race future,
Lorsque vous apprendrez la flétrissante injure

Qu'à ces arts désolés font des prêtres cruels?
   Un objet digne des autels
   Est privé de la sépulture!
Et dans un champ profane on jette à l'aventure
De ce corps si chéri les restes immortels!
Non, ces bords désormais ne seront plus profanes,
Ils contiennent ta cendre; et ce triste tombeau,
Honoré par nos chants, consacré par tes mânes,
   Est pour nous un temple nouveau!
Voilà mon Saint-Denys; oui, c'est là que j'adore
Tes talents, ton esprit, tes grâces, tes appas:
Je les aimai vivants, je les encense encore
   Malgré les horreurs du trépas,
   Malgré l'erreur et les ingrats,
Que seuls de ce tombeau l'opprobre déshonore.
Ah! verrai-je toujours ma faible nation,
Incertaine en ses voeux, flétrir ce qu'elle admire,
Nos moeurs avec nos loix toujours se contredire,
Et le Français volage endormi sous l'empire
   De la superstition?
   Quoi! n'est-ce donc qu'en Angleterre
   Que les mortels osent penser?
O rivale d'Athène, ô Londre! heureuse terre!
Ainsi que les tyrants vous avez su chasser
Les préjugés honteux qui vous livraient la guerre.
C'est là qu'on sait tout dire, et tout récompenser;
Nul art n'est méprisé, tout succès a sa gloire;
Le vainqueur de Tallard, le fils de la Victoire,
Le sublime Dryden, et le sage Addison,
Et la charmante Ophils, et l'immortel Newton,
   Ont part au Temple de Mémoire:
Et Lecouvreur à Londre aurait eu des tombeaux
Parmi les beaux-esprits, les rois, et les héros.
Quiconque a des talents, à Londre est un grand
  homme.
Le génie étonnant de la Grèce et de Rome,
Enfant de l'abondance et de la liberté,

Semble, après deux mille ans, chez eux ressuscité.
O toi, jeune Sallé, fille de Terpsichore,
Qu'on insulte à Paris, mais que tout Londre
    honore,
Dans tes nouveaux succès, reçois avec mes voeux
Les applaudissements d'un peuple respectable,
De ce peuple puissant, fier, libre, généreux,
Aux malheureux propice, aux beaux-arts favor-
    able.
Des lauriers d'Apollon dans nos stériles champs
La feuille négligée est-elle donc flétrie?
Dieux! pourquoi mon pays n'est-il plus la patrie
      Et de la gloire et des talents?

APPENDIX

Appendix

The following poems dedicated to the memory of Adrienne were not included in the main body of this work.

Epître à Mlle Lecouvreur
à propos de la dispute qui s'est élevée depuis quelque temps
au sujet de la déclamation des Dlles Duclos et Lecouvreur

Enfin le vrai triomphe et la fureur tragique
Fait place sur la scène au tendre, au pathétique,
C'est vous qui des douceurs de la simplicité
Nous avez fait connaître et sentir la beauté;
C'est vous qui, méprisant le prestige vulgaire,
Avez su vous former un nouvel art de plaire,
Vous dont les sons flatteurs, ignorés jusqu'alors,
Des passions de l'âme expriment les transports.
Avant que vous vinssiez, par Melpomène
    instruite,
D'un heureux naturel nous montrer le mérite,
Tel était de Paris le fol entêtement,
On donnait tout à l'art et rien au sentiment,
Et le théâtre en proie à des déclamatrices
N'offrait aux spectateurs que de froides actrices.
Un murmure confus s'élève contre moi,
Je porte le dégoût plus loin que je ne doi,
Le Théâtre-Français, en modèles fertile,
En sujets excellents ne fut jamais stérile

Rappelez-vous . . . de quoi prétend-on me
    blâmer?
Je ne conteste pas qu'on n'ait su déclamer.
Mais parvient-on au coeur par une voix forcée
Qui ne rend de l'auteur le sens ni la pensée?
Je ne m'en cache pas, il faut pour me flatter
M'émouvoir, m'attendrir et non m'épouvanter,
Je veux qu'on parle au coeur, et non pas aux
    oreilles,
Sans cela le Théâtre est pour moi sans merveilles,
Le plus pompeux récit est froid à me glacer.
Un mot succède à l'autre et le vient effacer.
Faut-il donc, pour toucher, des clameurs
    glapissantes,
Des gestes convulsifs, des écarts de Bacchantes?
Croit-on que je suis sourd? de grâce, calmez-vous;
Vous ne respirez plus, à quoi bon ce courroux?
Est-ce ainsi que s'exprime une jeune princesse
Que la crainte saisit, qu'agite la tristesse?
Quand par un seul regard qui déplut à l'Amour
L'imprudente Psyché le perdit sans retour,
Quand livrée au pouvoir de sa fière rivale
Malheureuse elle errait sur la rive infernale,
De ses tendres regards le charme et la douceur
De la Reine des morts adoucirent le coeur.
On ne l'entendit point dans les Royaumes sombres
Par de lugubres cris épouvanter les ombres.
Je ne suis point sensible à de fausses douleurs,
Et ce n'est qu'en pleurant qu'on m'arrache des
    pleurs.
La Nature et le coeur toujours d'intelligence
Veulent que tout soit simple, et l'excès les offense.
Je suis par des fureurs moins ému que surpris,
Je veux du pathétique, et n'entends que des cris.
Je ris quand je te vois, insensée Hermione,
Rappeler en criant l'ingrat qui t'abandonne.
Non, ce n'est point ainsi qu'on ramène un amant,
Il faut plus de tendresse et moins d'emportement,

Je sais que la douleur a peine à se contraindre,
Mais qui se plaint si haut ne paraît guère à
    plaindre.
Mon coeur n'est point de fer, il connaît l'amitié,
Le dépit, le soupçon, l'amour et la pitié.
De peine et de plaisir il est trop susceptible.
Je serais plus heureux si j'étais moins sensible.
Cependant avant vous je ne sentis jamais
Ces langueurs, ces transports et ces troubles
    secrets;
Douces émotions d'une âme pénétrée,
Vous seules de mon coeur avez trouvé
    l'entrée . . .
Mais que fais-je! pour prix d'avoir charmé mes
    sens,
N'ai-je à vous présenter que des vers languissants?
Quel tribut! je vous dois un hommage plus tendre,
C'est en vous écoutant que j'irai vous le rendre.

               Godard de Beauchamps.

L'Ombre de Racine à Mlle Lecouvreur: Epître

Depuis longtemps, aimable Lecouvreur,
Un poète estimé de vous et de la France
    Cherchait avec impatience
L'heureuse occasion de vous ouvrir son coeur
    Et par tendresse, et par reconnaissance.

Mes succès par vos soins surpassent mes désirs.
C'est par vous que Monime, Andromaque,
    Athalie,
     Phèdre, Roxane, Iphigénie,
      Heureux enfants de mes loisirs,
Vivent chez les Français, font encore leurs
    plaisirs.

Vos gestes, vos regards ont fait taire l'envie,
Et les vains sentiments des critiques jaloux,
Partagés autrefois, sont réunis par vous.

                         219

Jouissez, Lecouvreur, d'une gloire si belle.
    Ma reconnaissance et mon zèle
  Vous ont été cachés jusqu'à ce jour.
J'en rougis: il est temps de montrer du retour,
Et je vais, par ces vers faits au séjour des Ombres,
    Vous raconter le démêlé
Que sur vous, l'autre jour, dans nos bocages
    sombres
  Eut avec moi l'ingrate Champmeslé.

Mes soins et mon amour formèrent sa jeunesse.
N'avez-vous pas appris quelle fut ma tendresse
  Et ce qu'enfin pour elle j'ai souffert?
  Je lui disais que, vengeurs de ma flamme,
Apollon, Melpomène et l'Amour de concert
  Avaient fait naître une actrice charmante,
De grâces et d'esprit assemblage parfait,
  Telle en un mot que l'on vous représente,
Craint-on en vous louant de charger le
    portrait?
Chaque ombre que là-haut vos regards ont
    charmée
—Vous pouvez bien juger que le nombre en est
    grand—
    De mes discours zélé garant,
Vint joindre son suffrage à votre renommée.
Je lui dis que vos yeux, vos appas, vos talents
Ajoutaient à mes vers mille fois plus de charmes
Que par elle jadis mes poèmes naissants
Aux Français attendris n'arrachèrent de larmes,
Que vous seule en un mot, la même chaque jour,
    Et chaque jour inimitable,
    Possédiez l'art incomparable
D'inspirer la douleur et l'effroi tour à tour
Sans cesser un moment d'inspirer de l'amour.

Cet éloge à coup sûr devait m'être funeste,
  L'ombre irritée en frémit à l'instant.
Femme, rivale, actrice, on devine aisément

Si sa colère fut modeste.
Mais un heureux événement
L'interrompit, et m'épargna le reste.
Un Dieu—c'était l'Amour, ne vous étonnez pas
Que jusques aux Enfers il ait porté ses pas,
Il perce à votre nom les plus sombres
    retraites,—
L'Amour par vos attraits toujours sûr de ses
    coups
Préside également dans les lieux où vous êtes
    Et dans les lieux où l'on parle de vous.

Il arrive: sitôt qu'il frappe notre vue,
La foule d'habitants dans nos bois répandue
    Se rassemble de toutes parts.
    Ce Dieu découvre à nos regards
Un portrait que sa main avait pris soin de faire;
De trouble à son aspect je me sentis atteint,
Ce portrait enchanteur pouvait-il ne pas plaire?
    C'était le vôtre, et l'Amour l'avait peint.

Mais bientôt de ce Dieu la voix impatiente
Par un effort nouveau surpassa notre attente.
Il parle, le portrait obéit à ses loix:
On voit vos mouvements, on entend votre voix,
    On sent déjà la douce violence
    Qui va bientôt nous entraîner.
    Vous paraissez, l'Auditeur en silence
N'attend plus qu'un coup d'oeil pour se
    déterminer.

Il gémit avec vous, avec vous il s'irrite,
    Il se trouble, il tremble, il s'agite.
Un geste, un seul regard nous conduit tour à
    tour,
Du calme à la terreur, de la haine à l'Amour:
    Nous vous voyons cruelle, impétueuse,
        Tendre, fière, majestueuse,
Telle que dans Paris, charmant les spectateurs,
Vous enchantez les yeux et captivez les coeurs.

221

Ce spectacle aussitôt termina la querelle.
Plus surprise que nous, et vainement rebelle,
Champmeslé ressentit ce charme tout-puissant,
Vous admira, se tut, et fuit en rougissant.

Mais connaissez l'Amour, et quel est son empire.
Mon coeur, dans ce moment facile à s'enflammer,
Apprit en vous voyant qu'un ombre peut aimer,
Ou n'a pu résister au plaisir de le dire.
 Si mon hommage est d'un assez grand prix
Pour ne pas s'attirer un injuste mépris,
 Daignez répondre à mon impatience,
Daignez m'en témoigner quelque reconnaissance,
Le message est aisé, vous voyez quelquefois
Certain de mes amis qui dans sa jeune audace
Ne craint point d'aspirer au sommet du
  Parnasse;
Moi-même je le guide en ces sentiers étroits,
 Si vous voulez m'honorer d'une lettre,
 C'est dans ses mains qu'il faudra la remettre,
 Quoique pourtant je m'en fie à sa foi,
  Je ne sais quel trouble m'annonce
Que puisqu'il vous connaît, il pense comme moi;
Mais, fût-il mon rival, donnez-lui la réponse.

Le Franc de Pompignan.

A SELECTIVE
BIBLIOGRAPHY

A Selective Bibliography

AIGUEBERRE, DUMAS D'. *Seconde Lettre du souffleur de la Comédie de Rouen au garçon de café ou entretien sur les défauts de la déclamation*, ed. Jules Bonnassies. Paris: Willem, 1870.

AÏSSÉ, CHARLOTTE-ELISABETH, MLLE. *Lettres à Madame Calendrini*, ed. M. J. Ravenel. Paris: Gerdès, 1846.

ALEMBERT, JEAN LEROND D'. "Eloge historique de Marivaux," *Oeuvres philosophiques, historiques et littéraires*. Paris: Bastien, 1805. X, 219–280.

ALLAINVAL, LÉONOR-JEAN-CHRISTINE SOULAS, ABBÉ D'. *Lettre à Mylord *** sur Baron et la demoiselle Lecouvreur, où l'on trouve quelques particularités théâtrales, par George Wink (Abbé d'Allainval)*, ed. Jules Bonnassies. Paris: Willem, 1870.

ANON. *Mercure de France*, March, 1730, pp. 577–581.

————. "Nouvelles littéraires," *Mercure de France*, August, 1782, pp. 72–73.

Archives de la Bastille, ed. François Ravaisson. Paris: Pedone-Lauriel, 1883. XIV, 251–252.

ARGENTAL, CHARLES-AUGUSTIN DE FERRIOL D'. "Testament du comte d'Argental," *Archives historiques, artistiques et littéraires*, No. 3 (January 1, 1890), p. 129.

ASSE, EUGÈNE. "Les Filles d'Adrienne Lecouvreur," *Revue Rétrospective*, XVII (July–December, 1892), pp. 313–344.

BARBIER, EDMOND-JEAN-FRANÇOIS. *Journal (1861): chronique de la règne de Louis XV*. Paris: Charpentier, 1885. II, 94–97.

BATCHELDER, JOHN-DAVIS. *Drame d'Eugène Scribe "Adrienne*

Lecouvreur" et les influences de 1848. Paris: Société d'Imprimerie Française, 1909.

BEAUCHAMPS, GODARD DE. *Mémoires historiques et critiques.* Amsterdam: Bernard, 1722.

BERNHARDT, SARAH. *Adrienne Lecouvreur* (play in six acts). In *L'Illustration Théâtrale,* No. 65 (August 10, 1907).

BOINDIN, NICOLAS, attr. *Lettre historique sur tous les spectacles de Paris.* Paris: Prault, 1719.

BONNASSIES, JULES. *La Comédie-Française: histoire administrative (1658–1757).* Paris: Didier, 1874.

BONNEVAL, RENÉ DE. *Mémoires pour servir à l'histoire de la calotte.* Paris, 1732.

CAMPARDON, EMILE. *Les Comédiens du Roi de la troupe française.* Paris: H. Champion, 1875.

CASTRIES, RENÉ, DUC DE. *Maurice de Saxe 1696–1750.* Paris: Fayard, 1963.

Catalogue raisonné de l'oeuvre des Drevet, ed. anon. Paris: Didot, 1876.

Causes intéressantes avec les jugements qui les ont décidées, ed. anon. The Hague: Jean Néaulme, 1758.

CHARMOIS, LE VACHER DE. *Costumes et annales des grands théâtres de Paris.* Paris, 1758.

CLAIRON, CLAIR J. H. LEGRIS DE LATUDE, MLLE. *Mémoires.* Basle: Henricy, 1799.

CLÉMONT, JEAN-MARIE-BERNARD, and J. LAPORTE. *Anecdotes dramatiques.* Paris: Duchesne, 1775. III.

COLAUTTI, ARTURO. *Adriana Lecouvreur.* New York: Fred Rullman, 1962. (Libretto for opera by Francesco Cilea).

COLLÉ, CHARLES. *Journal et mémoires.* Paris: Didot, 1868. I, 140.

DELAUNAY DU GUÉ, AUNILLON, ABBÉ. *Mémoires de la vie galante, politique et littéraire.* Paris: Leopold Collin, 1808. I, 301–310; II, 1–6.

DIDEROT, DENIS. *Paradoxe sur le comédien.* In *Oeuvres,* ed. André Billy. Paris: Gallimard, 1951.

BIBLIOGRAPHY

Dussane, Béatrix. *La Comédie-Française.* Paris: Hachette, 1960.

Epinay, Louise-Florence-Pétrouille (Tardieu d'Esclavelles), Marquise d'. *Mémoires.* Paris: Charpentier, 1865. I, 213–217.

Esher, Reginald Baliol Brett, Viscount. "The Reverie of Adrienne," *Fasciculus J. W. Clark dictatus.* Cambridge, Eng., 1909, pp. 393–405.

Evans, George. "Petits portraits: Adrienne Lecouvreur," *La Société Nouvelle.* III (1914), 49–59.

Gay, Sophie, Mme. "Adrienne Lecouvreur," *Le Plutarque français,* ed. Edouard Mennechet. Paris: Crapelet, 1835: VII, notice No. 3.

Ginisty, Paul. *Mémoires et souvenirs de comédiennes.* Paris: Louis-Michaud, 1914.

Girault de Saint-Fargeau, Albert. *Les Quarante-huit quartiers de Paris.* Paris: Firmin, Didot, 1846.

Grouchy, Henri de, Vicomte. *Documents inédits relatifs à Jean Racine.* Paris: Techener, 1892.

Gueuillette, Charles. *Acteurs et actrices du temps passé.* Paris: Jouaust, 1881.

Jouin, Henri-Auguste. *Musée de portraits d'artistes: état de trois mille portraits.* Paris: Renouard, 1888.

Lagarde, Dubois de. "Lettre à M. ***," *Mercure de France,* February, 1760, pp. 126–127.

Lancaster, Henry Carrington. *French Tragedy in the Time of Louis XV and Voltaire, 1715–1774.* Baltimore: Johns Hopkins, 1950.

———. *The Comédie-Française 1701–1774.* In *Transactions of the American Philosophic Society,* XLI (December, 1951), 593–849.

La Place, A. J. de. *Pièces intéressantes et peu connues.* Paris: Prault, 1788. VI, 390–393.

Larroumet, Gustave. "Emile Lamé dans la revue *le Présent,*" *Revue d'Art Dramatique,* October 1, 1886.

LECOUVREUR, ADRIENNE. *Lettres,* ed. Georges Monval. Paris: Plon, 1892.

———. "Lettres à Maurice de Saxe," ed. Marquis d'Argenson. *Revue des Deux Mondes,* XXXVI (November–December, 1926), 804–842; XXXVII (January–February, 1927), 104–128, 349–371.

LECUYER-CORTHIS, GILBERTE. *Adrienne Lecouvreur.* Paris: Club de la Femme, 1960.

LE FRANC DE POMPIGNAN. O*euvres complètes de M. L*F****.* Paris, 1753.

LEMONTEY, PIERRE-EDOUARD. "Notice sur Adrienne Lecouvreur," *Oeuvres.* Paris: Sautelet, 1829. III, 321–347.

LEVY, BARBARA. *Adrienne.* New York: Holt, Rinehart Winston, 1960.

LOCK, FRÉDÉRIC. *Dictionnaire topographique et historique de l'ancien Paris.* Paris: Hachette, 1860.

LORENZ, PAUL. "Adrienne Lecouvreur," *Revue des Deux Mondes,* September 15, 1956, pp. 287–309.

LOUGH, JOHN. "A Paris Theatre in the Eighteenth Century," *University of Toronto Quarterly,* XXVII (1957–58), 289–304.

LYONNET, HENRI. *Les Comédiennes.* Paris: Marcel Seheur, 1929.

MANNE, EDOUARD-DENIS DE. *Galerie historique de la troupe de Voltaire.* Lyons: Scheuring, 1861.

MAY, GEORGES. *Diderot et "La Religieuse."* Paris: Presses Universitaires de France, 1954.

MESNARD, PAUL, ed. *Oeuvres de J. Racine.* Paris: Hachette, 1873. I.

MICHELET, JULES. *Histoire de France.* Paris: Flammarion, 1866. XV, 89–97.

OLIVIER, JEAN-JACQUES. *Voltaire et les comédiens.* Paris: Société Française d'Imprimerie, 1899.

PALÉOLOGUE, MAURICE. *Profils de femmes.* Paris: Calmann-Levy, 1895.

BIBLIOGRAPHY

Piron, Alexis. *Oeuvres complètes.* Paris: Rigoley de Juvigny, 1776.

Poisson, Philippe. "L'Actrice nouvelle," *Oeuvres.* Paris, 1766. II, 193–240.

Pollitzer, Marcel. *Grandes Actrices: leur vie, leurs amours.* Paris: La Colombe, 1958.

Racine, Louis. "Mémoires sur la vie et les ouvrages de Jean Racine," *Oeuvres complètes de Racine.* Paris: Editions du Seuil, 1962, pp. 1–87.

Recueil de poésies satiriques et des plus galantes tirées et choisies des milleurs auteurs, ed. anon. n.p., n.d.

Régistre 1717–1730. Paris: Archives de la Comédie-Française.

Régnier de la Brière, François-Joseph Pierre Tousey. *Souvenirs et études de théâtre.* Paris: Ollendorff, 1887, pp. 119–176.

Reuilly, Jean de. *La Raucourt et ses amies: étude historique des moeurs saphiques au 18e siècle.* Paris: Daragon, 1909.

Riccoboni, Luigi. *Dell'arte rappresentativa.* London: G. Riva, 1728.

Rivollet, Georges. *Adrienne Le Couvreur.* Paris: Félix Alcan, 1932.

Rogers, Cameron. *Gallant Ladies.* New York: Harcourt, Brace, 1928, pp. 259–295.

Rousseau, Jean-Jacques. *Lettre à d'Alembert sur les spectacles* (1758), ed. L. Brunet. Paris: Hachette, 1938.

Sainte-Beuve, Charles-Auguste de. "Adrienne Lecouvreur," *Causeries du Lundi.* Paris: Garnier, 1943. I, 199–220.

———. *Quelques Portraits féminins.* Paris: Tallandier, 1928.

Scribe, Eugène, and Ernest Legouvé. *Adrienne Lecouvreur* (play in five acts). Paris: Beck-Tresse, 1849.

Sorel, Cécile. *La Vie amoureuse d'Adrienne Lecouvreur.* Paris: Flammarion, 1925.

Stevenson, Florence. "Born for Tragedy," *Opera News,* February 9, 1963.

Titon du Tillet. "Eloge historique d'Adrienne Lecouvreur," *Supplément au Parnasse français,* 1743, pp. 806–810.

Troublet, Abbé de. "Lettre à M. de la Place," *Mercure de France,* April, 1760, pp. 113–115.

Voltaire, François-Marie Arouet de. *Voltaire's Correspondence,* ed. Theodore Besterman. Geneva, 1953–65.

———. "Epître à Mlle Le Couvreur," *Mercure de France,* December, 1723, p. 1129.

———. *Oeuvres complètes,* ed. Moland. Paris: Garnier, 1877–85.

———. *Oeuvres complètes,* ed. Beuchot. Paris: Lefèvre, 1829–40.

White, Jon Manchip. *Marshal of France.* London: Hamish Hamilton, 1962.

Index

INDEX